North Carolina's
ROADSIDE
EATERIES

D. G. MARTIN

North Carolina's

ROADSIDE EATERIES

A Traveler's Guide to Local Restaurants, Diners, and Barbecue Joints

REVISED AND EXPANDED EDITION

THE UNIVERSITY OF NORTH CAROLINA PRESS

Chapel Hill

A SOUTHERN GATEWAYS GUIDE

© 2024 D. G. Martin

Designed by Jamison Cockerham. Set in Chaparral, designed by
Carol Twombly; Voltage, designed by Laura Worthington; and Nelda,
designed by the Walden Font Company. Set by Rebecca Evans.

Cover photo by Donn Young. Unless otherwise noted,
all photographs by D. G. Martin.

Manufactured in the United States of America

ISBN 978-1-4696-6093-6 (pbk: alk. paper)
ISBN 978-1-4696-6094-3 (ebook)

The Library of Congress has cataloged the
original edition of this book as follows:
Names: Martin, D. G. (David Grier), 1940– author.
Title: North Carolina's roadside eateries : a traveler's guide to
    local restaurants, diners, and barbecue joints/by D. G. Martin.
Other titles: Southern gateways guide.
Description: Chapel Hill : The University of North Carolina Press, [2016] |
    Series: A Southern gateways guide
Identifiers: LCCN 2016019441 | ISBN 9781469630144 (pbk : alk. paper) |
    ISBN 9781469630151 (ebook)
Subjects: LCSH: Restaurants—North Carolina—Guidebooks. | Roads—
    North Carolina—Guidebooks.
Classification: LCC TX907.3.N8 M37 2016 | DDC 647.95756—dc23 LC record
    available at https://lccn.loc.gov/2016019441

Southern Gateways Guide™ is a registered trademark
of the University of North Carolina Press.

For Harriet Wall Martin; our children and their spouses,

Grier and Louise Martin and Cotton and May Bryan;

and our grandchildren, Sara Louise Martin, Margaret May Bryan,

Jacob Grier Bryan, and David Wall Bryan.

Contents

Foreword

"All great literature is one of two stories; a man goes on a journey or a stranger comes to town," wrote Russian writer Leo Tolstoy.

This little book may not be great literature, but it can open a way for you to make your own great stories, ones you can experience in your journeys along North Carolina highways when you become the stranger who comes to town to visit a local eatery and local people.

You can find information about more than 100 restaurants on the following pages. Still, this book is not primarily a book about food and certainly not a typical food guide. Rather, it is about community gathering places where food is also served.

If the book is successful, it will only be because it persuades you to do something different at mealtime when you are traveling, to be a journeying stranger and eat where locals come together.

The rewards will be bountiful memories. You will have stories you made for yourself, ones that you will remember long after you have forgotten stories other people wrote.

North Carolina's

ROADSIDE

EATERIES

Introduction to the
Second Edition

Many years ago, I began to write about my favorite country cooking places in my weekly newspaper column. My readers liked those columns better than my usual ones about politics and books. When I invited them to write about their favorite local haunts, I got enough material for more columns and for a series of magazine articles that featured local eateries near the interstates. All that led to the publication of the first edition of *Roadside Eateries* in 2016.

The food at these country cooking restaurants may not be fancy, but it is always good. No fancy chefs, but folks in the kitchen who have been cooking the dishes for many years. Our favorite places are local, comfortable, and welcoming.

Writing about these treasured eateries and assembling them into a timely book presents a special challenge. These places do not last forever. They go out of business, or change ownership, or keep chugging until they just run their natural course. It is sad to see them go, but there is also great joy in seeking and finding new and welcoming places to get sweet tea, some barbecue, or even good Chinese food. I love stopping at little diners that serve hushpuppies you never forget, meeting good folks, and watching people settle political differences over a slice of lemon pie. Sometimes I think I have seen and tasted nearly everything, but there will always be more. I love this state and love traveling its roads and have loved finding even more special places, and reporting back to you in this second edition.

Over time we lose some of our great favorites. We lost several that were featured in the first edition, including Wilber's in Goldsboro, Allen & Son in Chapel Hill, and Bill's in Wilson. These were special losses for all North Carolinians because they had become legendary gathering places.

The loss of these and others pushed me to go to work. I found substitutes for the lost classics and added a bunch of other good ones. By April 2020, I had a revised version completed and ready for publication that fall or the following winter. Amazon had already listed the revision and displayed the new cover on its website.

Then something happened—COVID.

Just as I was going over the final page proofs, I got a call from UNC Press. My editor, Lucas Church, said, "We don't know which of your restaurants can survive the battle against the virus. Let's talk about what we should do."

I understood and agreed. It was obvious that COVID was closing restaurants all over the country. We needed to delay publication, and we did. Though the book was on hold, we didn't stop working. We kept at it, getting ready for when it would be time to publish again.

That time is finally here.

The fractures we felt from the ever-present strain of politics on the state and national levels—coupled with the isolation most of us experienced during the COVID pandemic—reminded me how much I loved the experiences I know we all had in our favorite eateries, where people could gather, put differences aside, and eat as a community.

If this revised edition of *Roadside Eateries* contributes in any small way to our recovery from the painful disruptions of COVID and our broken politics, then we can be proud.

In this edition, I have added nearly forty new eateries. That's the good news.

The sad news, though, is the closure of some of my favorites, including several long-standing and beloved barbecue restaurants that closed their doors.

However, some that closed have been reborn. One was Wilber's, the iconic barbecue restaurant in Goldsboro, home of some of the best Eastern-style North Carolina barbecue around. Happily, Wilber's opened again but, unfortunately, too late to be included here. In the meantime, I have added nearby McCall's Bar-B-Que & Seafood, which has earned praises, even from some Wilber's loyalists.

Allen & Son Barbecue near I-40 and I-85 north of Chapel Hill also shut its doors. For many years, owner Keith Allen worked early and late to chop the hickory wood and manage the slow-cooked fire that brought pork shoulders to perfect eating condition. In its place, I have added Allen & Son Bar-B-Que—and, yes, it's a different restaurant! It is still open and thriving between Pittsboro and Chapel Hill on 15-501.

Bill's Barbecue near I-95 in Wilson closed after more than 55 years in business. Its founder, Bill Ellis, retired in 2015 and died in 2017. Even when Bill's 850 seats were full, visiting its bountiful buffet was like sitting down to a warm family meal. To fill this void, I have included Marty's BBQ, owned by Bill's son Lawrence, which gets great reviews from the people who loved his dad's offerings.

Carolina Bar-B-Q in Statesville, made famous by Charles Kuralt's cheerful criticism of the lean pork shoulder barbecue that lacked the fat and gristle he loved in whole hog 'cue, has also closed. Happily, that site is now occupied by Randy's BBQ, a worthy successor, one that Kuralt would enjoy and praise.

Similarly, the Lantern, one of my favorites in Dodson, closed several years ago. Thankfully, Noel and Julie Easter have moved their Central Cafe to the old Lantern restaurant location, bringing good meat-and-vegetable-plate options much like the Lantern.

Fuller's Old Fashioned Bar-B-Q in Lumberton was swept away by the floods that followed Hurricane Matthew. It has moved its operations to nearby Pembroke, taking the location of another one of my favorites, the now closed Sheff's Seafood, where I enjoyed great meals and fellowship when I worked at UNC-Pembroke a few years ago.

Holland's Shelter Creek Fish Camp near Burgaw was wonderfully located on the waters around the Cape Fear River. Sadly, it was flooded and destroyed. It has relocated to Holly Ridge north of Wilmington, a little too far from an interstate to be in the book. But still a great place for seafood.

But not every restaurant gets a new lease on life, even if it was a groundbreaker, like Nunnery-Freeman Barbecue in Henderson, where one of the best alternatives to wood-fired cooking was developed.

Sometimes it's not just the food I'll miss. The Snack Bar in Hickory was my model of a community gathering place where food was served cheerfully by a wait staff that had been there forever. It was home to the Liars Club, a group of retirees who gathered at about 6:30 for breakfast, then went home to rest awhile before coming back for coffee at about 10:30.

Same with Margaret's Cantina in Chapel Hill, a favorite of my daughter's family and, thus, a place where we have many good family memories. I miss it very much.

I'll also miss Linda's. When I worked as an interim official at UNC-Pembroke, it was an important place to meet and get to know some of the significant Lumbee people who were so welcoming to me.

In addition, we lost more of my favorites: Little Creek Cafe (Mars Hill), Judge's Riverside (Morganton), Smith Street Diner (Greensboro), Toot-N-Tell Restaurant (Garner), Dixie III Restaurant (Asheboro), Hill's Lexington Barbecue (Winston-Salem), Price's Chicken Coop (Charlotte), Acropolis Cafe & Grille (Cornelius), The Cook Shack (Union Grove), Wink's King of Barbecue and Richard's Bar-B-Q (Salisbury), Tommy's Bar-B-Que and Captain Tom's Seafood Restaurant (Thomasville), Angelo's Family Restaurant (Graham), Holt Lake Bar-B-Q & Seafood (Smithfield), and Broadnax Diner (Seaboard).

In this revised edition I have tried to follow the pattern set in the first edition by selecting restaurants that are local institutions and close enough to an interstate highway to be conveniently accessible to travelers. I have to confess that some of my selections are farther away from the highway than what you've seen before in *Roadside Eateries*, but in every case I believe the experience will be worth the extra miles.

In the coming months and years, I will be following the stories of the restaurants included in this edition, hoping they last forever but knowing that there will be changes and losses. I will have my eyes out for places I have missed and for those that will earn a place in any new edition. If you have suggestions, comments, or criticism, it would be great to hear from you at nceateries@yahoo.com.

But before we get into the great restaurants in this book—new and old—you might ask, "D. G., just where did you learn that local restaurants are where you find real friends and lifelong memories?"

Maybe it was my North Mecklenburg High School football teammate Tommy Oehler who got me started when he introduced me to his dad, J. W., and the wonders of the annual Mallard Creek Church barbecue, which the Oehler family still manages every October north of Charlotte. There is no better example of how good barbecue and a host of friendly people make a meal into something memorable.

My whole life, to this day, I've been on the lookout for places where I can find the Mallard Creek feeling. The places I've found that live up to Mallard Creek, at least in my mind—the restaurants that are about food, friends, and more—are the places you'll find in this book. So when I'm asked just where I learned that local restaurants are where you find real friends and lifelong memories, I suppose my answer would be: North Carolina. I have a lifetime's worth of memories about the food and friendship in this state, and they led me to write this book.

When I moved to Chapel Hill to work for the late University of North Carolina System president Dick Spangler, he introduced me to Breadmen's, where the great and bountiful servings of solid food and the ever presence of policemen and community leaders made it my second home until my wife joined me in Chapel Hill. Now, she and I take our grandchildren there and spoil them with pancakes and french fries while we still split the giant vegetable plate, almost always choosing the tasty banana pudding, which Breadmen's includes as one of the veggie options—even though everybody knows it's not a vegetable. But I wanted to know about other country cooking places. Jack Hunt, a powerful legislator from Cleveland County, was married to a cousin of President Spangler, who told me I could go to Jack if I ever needed help in my work with the legislature. So one day I did ask him for help: "Where is the best place to get country cooking around here?"

He paused, squinted, smiled a little bit, and finally said, "Well, the truth is there is nothing better, I think, than Ruby's cooking." His wife, Spangler's cousin, was the Ruby in question. Jack and Ruby regularly invited their government friends for informal suppers of country ham, baked chicken, cornbread, biscuits with sourwood honey and molasses, and vegetables from her garden, including corn frozen minutes after it was picked the previous summer. There were always desserts of homemade cakes and pies. Of course, there was also the opportunity to make friends with governors, Supreme Court justices, and legislative leaders.

Once, when President Spangler and Governor Jim Hunt were at loggerheads about the governor's budget proposals for the university, they could hardly speak to each other until Jack invited them to breakfast with Ruby. Neither the governor nor the university president could say no to Ruby. It was only after they sat down to Ruby's cooking and warm spirit that they worked out a compromise.

Some of the other lobbyists had resources to entertain legislators at fancy and expensive restaurants. I had no expense account. But I found that I could always get wonderful and inexpensive country cooking and run into important legislators at places such as Big Daddy's and Finch's, where the food was great, the servers were friendly, and the atmosphere was warm and inclusive enough to be conducive to building trust.

On one occasion, university vice president the late Bill McCoy and I left from Chapel Hill about noon, driving to Cullowhee for a meeting at Western Carolina University. By the time we were approaching Winston-Salem on I-40, McCoy said he was getting hungry for a barbecue sandwich. I quickly agreed but admitted that I did not know where there was a good place to stop. We called the law offices of the late Ham Horton, then serving in the legislature and a well-known food fan. Horton was unavailable, his receptionist told us, because he was in an important real estate closing.

"Tell him we only need him for a minute because we need a place to eat," we pled. Thankfully, Horton came to the phone and quickly gave us a recommendation and directions.

It was at that moment that the seeds for this guidebook were planted.

I left the university in the fall of 1997 to run for the U.S. Senate. After I was soundly defeated in the primary by John Edwards, Chancellor Joseph Oxendine at UNC-Pembroke asked me to work for him for 6 months. While I was there, he introduced me to Lumbee Indian culture and two of his favorite restaurants: Linda's, where the lunchtime crowd of locals politely welcomed the "university crowd" to join them for lunch, and Shef's, where the seafood suppers drew people from all over Lumbee Land.

A few months after that assignment ended, North Carolina Central University chancellor Julius Chambers asked me to work for him for a few months. I enjoyed eating with my staff at the faculty cafeteria; it was not a regular restaurant, of course, but the country food was delicious. One day the special plate was pigs' feet. I remember how everybody looked over to see how I was going to deal with that dish. I pretended that I did not notice their looks and cleaned my plate and ate all the meat and tasty fat from every toe.

Folks at Central introduced me to Dillard's, where people from all over Durham gathered to enjoy barbecue with a mustard-based sauce more like they serve in South Carolina. Sadly, Dillard's closed a few years ago. While in Durham, I met some of my Central staff at Bullock's Bar-B-Cue in Durham, described later in this book.

Meanwhile, another interim job with the Trust for Public Land took me back to Charlotte for more than a year. I introduced my staff to the Open Kitchen, which was the same as it was so many years earlier. They introduced me to Lupie's Cafe, where we gathered for simple but tasty fare and the chance to meet people from all over town. Both these great places are described in this book. Unfortunately, another of my Charlotte favorites, Anderson's, home of the World's Best Pecan Pie and where I spent many happy mornings at business, political, church, and social gatherings, closed a few years ago.

But that is the challenge of writing about restaurants: they have a life span. They come, they go. But part of the joy in all these jobs I've had over the years and all the traveling I've done is finding new and welcoming places to pull up, grab a seat, and talk with good folks while eating wonderful North Carolina home cooking.

I've written for years about these places and published books and countless columns about them and the people who run them. I hope you enjoy what's ahead in this book and that it inspires you to go a little out of your way to find something special, where the folks will likely greet you like an old friend, even if it's your first visit.

INTERSTATE 26

In one of the most beautiful sections of our state, this highway runs from the mountain border with eastern Tennessee through Asheville, Hendersonville, and Saluda and then down to the South Carolina line. I-26 opens the door for its travelers to make a quick visit to an eatery in a mountain holler or a small college town or other mountain towns where tourists and local mountain people sit down together for good, solid meals.

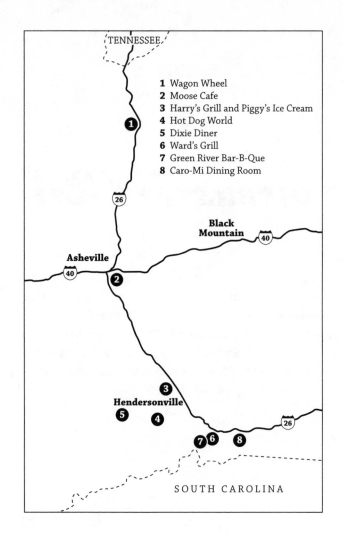

··

Wagon Wheel

390 Carl Eller Road, Mars Hill, NC 28754 · (828) 689-4755
Tuesday–Saturday 6:00 A.M.–2:00 P.M.

For more than 10 years, Wagon Wheel owner Camille Metcalf has been serving breakfast, lunch, and supper to her regular customers in Mars Hill—and to tourists. She gives them a hearty breakfast, lunch specials with everything included for about $6, and dinner for well under $10. And for the kids and college students there are always burgers, fries, and homemade pies.

FROM I-26 Take Exit 11 and follow NC 213 toward Mars Hill for about 1 mile. Wagon Wheel is on the left.

AFTER EATING Take a walk on the lovely campus of Mars Hill University. Some of the action in Ron Rash's novel *The Cove* is set in the town and on the campus during World War I. Rash was asked once why North Carolina produces so many good authors and so many good stories. He said, "This is what North Carolinians do. We do barbecue and novels."

Other eateries in the area are described in the I-40 chapter, including Little Pigs Bar-B-Q, Luella's Bar-B-Que, and 12 Bones Smokehouse.

· ·

Moose Cafe

570 Brevard Road #3, Asheville, NC 28806 · (828) 255-0920
Open every day 7:00 A.M.–8:00 P.M.
eatatthemoosecafe.com

It is always a great thing to hear about other people's favorite gathering and eating places. Sandra Arscott wrote to tell me about the Moose Cafe near the Farmers Market in Asheville. She bragged about the homemade biscuits and cornbread. She loves the Moose Cafe's apple butter so much that she always buys jars of it to take home. She told me about the iced tea served in mason jars. She wrote about the great mountain views from the restaurant's windows, including a wonderful look at the Biltmore House.

Based on her recommendation, I persuaded my Asheville friend John Curry to eat supper with me there. He ordered one of the special meat-and-two-vegetables plates. "It's delicious," he said, "but it's too much. I can't eat it all." Because I was hungry from a mountain hike, I ordered the "Country Feast." It costs a few dollars more but

Moose Cafe
in Asheville

allowed me to order all the meat and vegetables I could eat, plus dessert. Just to be sure that their mashed potatoes, cabbage, collards, carrots, pinto beans, and other vegetables were as "Farmers Market fresh" as Sandra Arscott promised, I sampled them all. And Sandra was right. They were fresh and cooked "just right."

I asked John Curry a question I always raise on my search for eateries: "Is the restaurant a community gathering place, where local people come to meet and catch up with their friends?" John nodded, smiled, and pointed across the way to his friends Doug and Laura Manofsky, who were eating supper with two of their children. "Oh, yes, it's a place where all kinds of Asheville folks come," Doug said. "We got started a few years ago when the contractor who was building our new home recommended the Moose Cafe. We've been eating here regularly ever since."

If I lived in Asheville, I would be eating there regularly, too. Instead, I will have to wait until the next time I am traveling nearby. But I will not have to wait until then to sample some of the Moose's best food. On the way out, John Curry and I stopped at the small gift shop inside the café. We studied the selection of T-shirts and souvenirs and were tempted by the handmade pottery, blankets, and rocking chairs that nearby mountain craftspeople leave for the Moose to display and sell. But like Sandra Arscott had written me, the gift shop's most popular item is Moose's apple butter, and John Curry bought me a couple of jars to take home and enjoy until I am back on I-26 again.

FROM I-26 Take Exit 33 (NC 191 North/Brevard Rd.). Follow Brevard Rd. north toward Asheville and the Farmers Market for 1.5 miles. The Moose Cafe is on the right just before you reach the Farmers Market.

FROM I-40 Take Exit 47 and follow signs to the Farmers Market.

AFTER EATING Wander in the restaurant's store for the apple butter and other gift ideas. Then find your way to the nearby Farmers Market to see what is in season.

. . . .

Harry's Grill and Piggy's Ice Cream

102 Duncan Hill Road, Hendersonville, NC 28792 · (828) 692-1995
Hours vary by season; call or check website before you go.
harrysandpiggys.com

What are an ice cream shop and a grill doing under the same roof? I asked myself that question as I stood in line to place my order at Harry's Grill and looked across the way at a separate line of folks waiting to order ice cream at Piggy's.

I sat down in one of the booths and began to examine the items hanging on the walls all around—signs from Howard Johnson's,

Wall Drug in South Dakota, and an old Esso station. There were Ronald McDonald and Big Boy statues. License tags from across the country, pictures, and all sorts of memorabilia covered every inch of the surrounding walls. Just what is going on here? I wondered again. It did not take me long to find the answer.

Mrs. "Piggy" Thompson, the owner of Harry's, Piggy's, and all the statues and signs on the wall, sat down at my booth and answered all my questions. "Back in 1980, when my late husband, Harry, told me he was going to start an ice cream stand here, I told him that I sure was not going to run it. But, when it was time to open up, Harry was still working at his regular job, and there was no one else to run it. So guess what? I came down here and started dipping ice cream, by myself—just like I said I would not do. We started with more than 20 flavors of Biltmore ice cream. Business gradually grew and grew. We did so well that pretty soon Harry decided he wanted to start a restaurant right here in the same place. Harry died while the restaurant's addition was still under construction. But we opened it in 1993 and, of course, named it after him. My sons Jeff and Todd are helping me now. In fact, they are doing most everything. Another son, Michael, who is a lawyer in Hendersonville, still comes by every now and then to help us dip ice cream. We are really proud of our barbecue. We smoke it with wood, and we offer a tomato-based sauce that we think is real good. We do have just one customer who says our barbecue is the best, but he brings his own sauce."

Piggy Thompson noticed that I was looking at a Howdy Doody figure on the wall. "Buffalo Bob himself once came by to buy ice cream and autographed it for us," she explained. "We've had some other celebrities to drop by. When I heard Perry Como had a place in Saluda, I invited him to come by for some ice cream, complimentary of course. But guess what? When he came, I wasn't here and the girls at the counter charged him for it just like everyone else. They didn't know who he was. That was hard for me to believe."

She told me that although the business increases in the summer, with tourists and lots of visits from the summer camps in the area, about 75 percent of their customers are always local. "We never did any advertising," she said, "never needed to." Even if the barbecue and ice cream were not so good and the memorabilia on the walls was not so interesting, I would come back here just to have another visit with Piggy Thompson.

FROM I-26   Take Exit 49 (US 64 West/Hendersonville). Follow US 64 West toward Hendersonville for about 1 mile until it intersects with Dana Rd. Turn right on Dana Rd. (which becomes Duncan Hill Rd.). Go about one block, and after crossing E. 7th Ave., you will see Harry's and Piggy's on the right. They are across Duncan Hill Rd. from Lowe's.

AFTER EATING   Just down the street, at 235 Duncan Hill Rd., is the Music Academy of Western North Carolina. Give them a call at (828) 693-3726 to let them know you are coming and maybe they will be able to show you some of their highly praised facilities.

· ·

Hot Dog World

226 Kanuga Road, Hendersonville, NC 28739 · (828) 697-0374
Monday–Saturday 10:00 A.M.–4:00 P.M., closed Sunday
NO CREDIT CARDS
hotdogworld.net

At Hot Dog World, located near downtown Hendersonville, Steve Katsadouros has been serving hot dogs for more than 30 years. Born in Greece in 1972, he grew up in Charlotte and graduated from UNC–Chapel Hill in 1982. Steve and his wife, Dora, bought Hot Dog World from her father and made it the go-to place for great hot dogs in western North Carolina. Amazingly, they sell 6,000 to 7,000 hot dogs every week, and locals line up to buy them.

The local favorite is the slaw dog, with mustard, chili, onion, and slaw on top, though they're happy to have customers order it however they like it. They toast their buns and use a special bun that they open on top.

Steve's Greek background opened the door to adding Greek salads and gyro sandwiches to the menu, along with other American favorites, such as milkshakes and hamburgers. It's a lively and inviting place, where tourists can mingle with the locals and get a chance to visit with Steve, Dora, long-time employee and partner Thanasi Tsakalos, or servers like Wendy, who has worked there for almost 30 years.

DIRECTIONS Take Exit 49B onto Four Seasons Blvd. (US 64 West) toward downtown Hendersonville. Continue traveling until you reach N. Church St. (US 25). Turn left onto Church St. Take a right onto Kanuga Rd. Hot Dog World is on the left, just past the Chamber of Commerce.

AFTER EATING Visit the Henderson County Heritage Museum in the former courthouse building a few blocks away. They're open Wednesday–Saturday 10:00 A.M.–5:00 P.M. and Sunday 1:00 P.M.–5:00 P.M. Admission is free, and their phone number is (828) 694-1619.

. . . .

Dixie Diner

1724 Brevard Road, Hendersonville, NC 28791 · (828) 697-5025
Monday–Sunday 7:00 A.M.–2:00 P.M.

Even if the food wasn't excellent (and it is), Hendersonville locals would still support owner Vickie Olek for providing a breakfast buffet for veterans and Servicemen and -women on the third Thursday of every month. Sometimes as many as eighty vets show up and have a delicious breakfast, which Olek and a local nonprofit cover.

"It's a really good feeling," she told a local television station. "These guys deserve this. This might be the only time they get to talk to someone else you know."

The decor is simple and the parking lot crowded, but as one visitor put it, there is plenty of good food: chocolate chip pancakes, eggs Benedict, country ham biscuits, banana pecan short stack, corned beef hash platter, and raspberry-stuffed French toast or cranberry waffles served with orange-infused syrup.

FROM I-26 Take Exit 49B onto US 64 West, and go about 2 miles. Turn left onto Buncombe St., then turn right onto 6th Ave. West. Continue onto US 64 West/Brevard Rd. Dixie Diner will be on your left.

AFTER EATING Make the 5-minute drive from the Dixie Diner to Tom's Park for a picturesque and dog-friendly place to walk and play shuffleboard.

. . . .

Ward's Grill

24 Main Street, Saluda, NC 28773 · (828) 749-2321
Tuesday–Saturday 8:00 A.M.–3:00 P.M.;
closed Sunday and Monday
thompsons-store.com

Even if you're not hungry for home cooking, you should stop in Saluda, one of North Carolina's most charming small towns and just a couple of miles off the interstate. Saluda is the home of the Orchard Inn, one of the finest bed-and-breakfasts I have ever visited. The Purple Onion cafe and coffee house on Main Street is a favorite of mine—but not for home cooking. It has an upscale California-type menu, with modest North Carolina prices.

But if you want country cooking for breakfast or lunch, surrounded by old-time local people, take a walk down Main Street and stop at Ward's Grill. On my last visit, while I was sitting at one of its small tables sipping a cup of coffee with my hamburger "all the way," I thought for a moment that I had been transported back in time about 50 years.

Current owner Clark Thompson explained how the history of Ward's Grill goes back a long way. George Lafatte Thompson first opened Thompson's Store in Saluda in 1890, which makes it the oldest grocery store still in existence in North Carolina. His daughter, Lola Thompson Ward, took over the store from her father in the late 1930s. Husband Roy Ward encouraged her to open the grill next door in 1960, which became the Ward's Grill we know today.

Charlie Ward, one of their sons, created the recipe for his famous "Charlie's Sage Sausage" in the 1940s. It is still made fresh daily, using the same recipe and sausage grinder for more than 75 years. The sausage is served in the grill as well as sold in the store's meat market. After declining health forced Charlie to sell the two businesses in 2008 and a short period of ownership by others, current owner Clark Thompson stepped in. Clark explained, "Charlie's widow, Judy, and I teamed up to bring the store and grill back into the family, reopening the grill in July 2010 and Thompson's Store in January 2011. Judy is a minor business partner and manager for the store. Melissa Wood, who had run her own grill in a nearby community for 10 years, manages the grill."

I still remember the hamburger from my visit, as I looked up at the high ceilings, listened to the onions sizzling on the grill, and thought to myself that this was a better look at times gone by than any museum could ever provide.

Charlie was right. The fresh meat from Thompson's next door gave my hamburger a good start. But it was the chili Charlie bragged about that made the whole thing a perfect treat. Clark Thompson says they have gone one better. "One very popular addition to Ward's Grill menu is our CJ burger, which is a 50-50 mixture of our own Charlie's Famous Sage Sausage and fresh ground chuck. Customers love them. And at lunch Melissa's cornbread salad, cold slaw, potato salad, tuna salad, and cobblers are also more than worthy of writing home about."

FROM I-26 Take Exit 59 (Saluda) and follow the signs toward Saluda, traveling Louisiana Ave. (Ozone Rd.) for 1 mile to US 176. Turn right on US 176 (Main St.), then go 0.5 mile into Saluda.

AFTER EATING Visit the historic Thompson's Store next door, open daily from 8:00 A.M. until 6:00 P.M. (6:30 on Saturday) and on Sunday from 11:00 A.M. to 4:00 P.M. during the summer.

Green River Bar-B-Que

131 US 176, Saluda, NC 28773 · (828) 749-9892
Sunday–Thursday 11:00 A.M.–8:00 P.M.;
Friday–Saturday 11:00 A.M.–9:00 P.M.
greenriverbbq.com

For almost 25 years, Melanie Talbot has been serving Eastern-style North Carolina barbecue to western North Carolinians. And they love it. Along with a small pork plate for about $10, she will give you three sides, including, if you want, some that you will not find other places, like tomato pie, Vidalia onion slaw, sweet potato fries, or corn nuggets with creamed corn in the middle. No wonder it is a popular gathering place for Saluda residents and tourists from all over.

FROM I-26 Take Exit 59 and follow the signs to Saluda, traveling Louisiana Ave. (Ozone Rd.) for 1 mile to US 176. Turn right on US 176 (Main St.) into Saluda, and just over the bridge Green River will be on your left.

AFTER EATING Make your way back to Main St. and explore the town's history of the railroad over the years.

Caro-Mi Dining Room

3231 US 176, Tryon, NC 28782 · (828) 859-5200
Wednesday–Friday 5:00 P.M.–8:00 P.M.;
Saturday 4:00 P.M.–8:00 P.M.; closed Sunday–Tuesday
NO CREDIT CARDS
caro-mi.com

On the porch of the Caro-Mi just outside Tryon, you can wait for a wonderful meal while listening to the rushing sounds of the Pacolet River as it flows by. Charles Stafford, a former teacher and school administrator, has owned Caro-Mi since 1990. He is proud that two of North Carolina's leading food experts tout his restaurant—for different reasons.

Jim Early, author of *The Best Tar Heel Barbecue: Manteo to Murphy*, raves about the skillet-fried chicken livers and mountain trout, along with the vinegar-based shredded coleslaw.

Bob Garner, of UNC-TV and *Our State* magazine fame, recommends especially the old-fashioned, North Carolina, "climate cured" country ham served here. Other friends also tell me about the country ham that the owners call "The Ham What Am."

FROM I-26 Take Exit 67 (NC 108/Tryon). Follow NC 108 toward Tryon for 2.3 miles until it meets Harmon Field Rd. Bear right and follow Harmon Field Rd. for 0.7 mile, where it intersects with US 176. Turn right on US 176 and follow it for about 2 miles. Caro-Mi is on the left.

AFTER EATING Sit on the porch of the Caro-Mi and listen to the rushing sounds of the North Pacolet River flowing by, on its way to South Carolina and the Broad and Santee Rivers and on to the Atlantic Ocean. There are different stories about the source of the Pacolet name. Some say it means "swift horse" in Cherokee. Others say it means "swift messenger" in French. The logo of the former Pacolet Mills in South Carolina featured a "swift horse."

INTERSTATE 40

I suppose driving from the eastern part of the state to the mountains these days is a lot better than it used to be.

After all, instead of driving on the curvy two-lane roads that took us through Valdese, Morganton, Marion, and Old Fort, we just drive along four-lane I-40. And if there are no traffic jams, we can just cruise along the entire way without stopping.

Well, maybe it's better than it used to be, maybe it's not. Come to think of it, I enjoyed some of the times on those old highways, riding through these mountain towns and sometimes stopping to eat a real meal in a local restaurant.

Most North Carolinians know that you can travel from Wilmington to California without hitting a stoplight if you stay on I-40. But if you are leaving North Carolina for California or other points west, you ought not to go without having a meal in the company of some real North Carolinians. If you are traveling west of Asheville, keep reading, because I have found some great spots for home cooking that will help you remember our state until you return.

Following the 420 miles of I-40 that take you from the Tennessee line to Wilmington, you can visit every region of our state and drive by most of its major cities. You will also have the opportunity to eat the same barbecue Barack Obama did, to find it cooked and sauced many different ways in addition to the Lexington and Eastern styles, and to be amazed at the bountiful all-you-can eat buffets in Eastern North Carolina's rural communities.

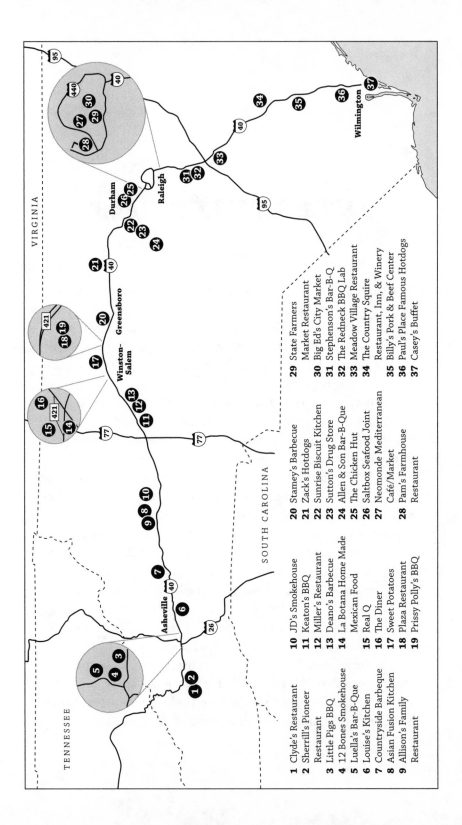

TENNESSEE

VIRGINIA

SOUTH CAROLINA

Asheville

Winston-Salem

Greensboro

Durham

Raleigh

Wilmington

1 Clyde's Restaurant
2 Sherrill's Pioneer Restaurant
3 Little Pigs BBQ
4 12 Bones Smokehouse
5 Luella's Bar-B-Que
6 Louise's Kitchen
7 Countryside Barbeque
8 Asian Fusion Kitchen
9 Allison's Family Restaurant
10 JD's Smokehouse
11 Keaton's BBQ
12 Miller's Restaurant
13 Deano's Barbecue
14 La Botana Home Made Mexican Food
15 Real Q
16 The Diner
17 Sweet Potatoes
18 Plaza Restaurant
19 Prissy Polly's BBQ
20 Stamey's Barbecue
21 Zack's Hotdogs
22 Sunrise Biscuit Kitchen
23 Sutton's Drug Store
24 Allen & Son Bar-B-Que
25 The Chicken Hut
26 Saltbox Seafood Joint
27 Neomonde Mediterranean Café/Market
28 Pam's Farmhouse Restaurant
29 State Farmers Market Restaurant
30 Big Ed's City Market
31 Stephenson's Bar-B-Q
32 The Redneck BBQ Lab
33 Meadow Village Restaurant
34 The Country Squire Restaurant, Inn, & Winery
35 Billy's Pork & Beef Center
36 Paul's Place Famous Hotdogs
37 Casey's Buffet

Now, it can be difficult to find good mom-and-pop places to get a good meal and meet the locals, what with all the overwhelming number of fast food options out there, but don't worry. I've found some great local restaurants for you to try. If you like good old-fashioned barbecue, hot dogs with a history, or some of the best Laotian food in the country, keep on reading.

· ·

Clyde's Restaurant

2107 S. Main Street, Waynesville, NC 28786 · (828) 456-9135
Wednesday–Sunday 11:00 A.M.–9:00 P.M.;
closed Monday and Tuesday

Clyde's is a favorite memory of novelist and expert on perfumes Sarah Colton, a native of Asheville who now lives in Paris, where she still thinks about the chocolate pie she ate at Clyde's growing up. It is still on the menu. Others say the lemon pie is even better. In its "Best Kept Secrets," series, the *News and Observer* compared Clyde's with a fancier restaurant and wrote, "We were happier with the fare at Clyde's Restaurant, a bustling comfort-food diner. Pretty good fried chicken, mac and cheese, and a generous salad."

Clyde's is about 10 miles from I-40, but it may be your last chance, or first opportunity, to get North Carolina home cooking on the way to or from the Tennessee line.

FROM I-40 Take Exit 27 (US 19-23 South) toward Waynesville for about 10 miles into Waynesville. Take Exit 98 and turn left onto Hyatt Creek Rd., and then immediately take a left onto S. Main St.

AFTER EATING Follow S. Main St. into the center of Waynesville, which was the model for the town of Cold Mountain in Charles Frazier's novel.

Sherrill's Pioneer Restaurant

8363 Carolina Boulevard, Clyde, NC 28721 · (828) 627-9880
Monday–Saturday 5:00 A.M.–8:00 P.M.; closed Sunday

Dean Sherrill's family has been running the Pioneer for as long as anybody can remember. Always a family affair, Dean, his brother, and their mother operated it for many years. More recently, Dean Sherrill and his wife, Lisa, have run the Pioneer with the help of a lot of family members. Now their children are taking charge.

Local folks crowd into the small restaurant and fill its 10 booths and all the counter space for breakfast and lunch. Travelers experience a trip back in time to the America of the 1950s. They see signs on the wall like "If we don't take care of our customer . . . somebody else will." Try the homemade vegetable beef soup, a bargain. At lunch and dinner, locals love the meat-and-three-vegetables specials.

FROM I-40 Take Exit 27 (connector to US 19-23-74). Continue for about 1.5 miles. Then bear left and follow signs to US 19-23 North into Clyde, which becomes Carolina Blvd. Sherrill's is on the right.

AFTER EATING Drive a few blocks to get a look at the Pigeon River (named for the extinct passenger pigeons that used the river to guide their migration). Or make your way into downtown Clyde and visit stores like Old Grouch's Military Surplus, which the Veteran-Owned Business organization says "is the largest, most knowledgeable and best stocked military surplus store in Western North Carolina. A real, traditional military surplus store with actual military surplus." You can check out the store's stock in advance at store. oldgrouch.biz.

Another eatery in the area, the Moose Cafe,
is described in the I-26 chapter.

Little Pigs Bar-B-Q

384 McDowell Street, Asheville, NC 28803 · (828) 254-4253
Monday–Saturday 10:30 A.M.–8:00 P.M.; closed Sunday
littlepigsbbq.net

Our friends Margie and Tom Haber live in Chapel Hill now, and they know something about fine dining in expensive restaurants. Their nephew, Hunter Lewis, has been a writer and editor at *Bon Appétit*, *Southern Living*, and *Cooking Light*. But they grew up in Asheville, and their eyes get a little misty when they talk about Little Pigs Bar-B-Q in their hometown. "It has been around since we were teenagers and it was just up the street from Lee H. Edwards High School (now Asheville High School), and that is where all the high school kids went after school. And the Swicegoods are still there, aren't they?"

Peggy and Joe Swicegood were together for more than 60 years, counting courtship and marriage, until Joe died in 2018. Both came to work every day to help their managers, Bruce Gordon and Matt Thomas. Until his passing, Joe worked the lines to make sure his customers are happy even when they have to wait.

Although the barbecue is still the main draw and Bruce and Matt cook 60 to 70 pork shoulders every week, the pressure-fried or broasted chicken is also very tasty and very popular. After eating several pieces, *Cold Mountain* author Charles Frazier said that he was taking Little Pigs' chicken to his next Inman family reunion.

FROM I-40 Take Exit 50 toward US 25 North. Follow US 25 North (Hendersonville Rd., All Souls Crescent St., and McDowell St.) for about 2 miles. Little Pigs is on the right.

AFTER EATING Cross the street and walk on the campus of historic Asheville High School. Its alumni, in addition to the Habers, include famed UNC and professional football player Charlie Justice and noted author Marisha Pessl, who has appeared on UNC-TV's *North Carolina Bookwatch*.

12 Bones Smokehouse

5 Foundy Street, Suite 10, Asheville, NC 28801 · (828) 253-4499
Monday–Friday 11:00 A.M.–4:00 P.M.; closed Sunday–Monday
12bones.com

Even if 12 Bones had not been made famous by Barack Obama's visits there, it would be a "must-do" in Asheville. Thomas Montgomery and Sabra Kelly opened 12 Bones in the Riverside area in 2005. In 2012 they sold the restaurant to Bryan King and Angela Koh King, who have continued the reputation for making everything from scratch. Bryan grew up in Spruce Pine and Asheville. After college at North Carolina State and travel in Asia, he moved to San Francisco, where he met Angela, who grew up in Iowa. Her father escaped from North Korea as a child, which is a story in itself. When 12 Bones went on the market, Angela and Bryan moved to Asheville, learned every position in 12 Bones, and have continued its success. Now, as experienced operators, they say, "We believe that simple ingredients and lots of care in preparation make the best food."

When my group visited, John Curry got a vegetable plate with baked beans, corn pudding, and collards. The rest of us feasted on the signature 12-boned ribs, delicious and addictive, smoked with cherry wood coals. Other dishes set 12 Bones apart from the usual North Carolina barbecue, but the ribs are very special.

Bryan and Angela also do a booming business at their Arden location at 2350 Hendersonville Rd.

FROM I-40 Take Exit 50 for US 25 toward S. Asheville for 0.3 mile. Turn left onto US 25 North/Hendersonville Rd. (pass by Bank of America Financial Center, on the right in 0.6 miles). Use the left 2 lanes to turn slightly left onto All Souls Crescent (pass by Starbucks on the left). Continue onto McDowell, then turn left onto Short McDowell St. Turn right onto Meadow Rd., then continue on to Lyman St. and drive to Foundy St. Continue straight onto Lyman St. and turn right onto Old Lyman St. 12 Bones Smokehouse will be on the left.

AFTER EATING Take a stroll through the surrounding River Arts District and visit art and craft studios (find more at ashevillerad.com), or take a few minutes to watch the nearby French Broad drift by.

···

Luella's Bar-B-Que

501 Merrimon Avenue, Asheville, NC 28804 · (828) 505-7427
Sunday–Thursday 11:00 A.M.–9:00 P.M.;
Friday–Saturday 11:00 A.M.–10:00 P.M.
luellasbbq.com

Katherine Frazier and her husband, Charles, introduced me to Luella's, one of their favorites. Maybe they like it so much because Luella's treasures its history and family connections. Owner and "pit boss" Jeff Miller explains that the restaurant is named after his grandmother, who "did all the cooking when the family would get together for Sunday dinner and holidays. Scratch cooking from the garden at its best. What she handed down was an understanding of how great food is created—honest good cooking, made with a loving hand." Jeff tries to follow that tradition, using local foods and giving a variety of options in addition to his highly praised barbecue. Or, as he brags, "Made-from-scratch, high-quality grub, tasting great every day."

At lunchtime, one patron, Brian Ross, bragged about the wings ("smoked for two hours and fried") and the ribs and "the Bloody Marys on Sundays." Customer Kate Ross told me she prefers the simple salad with a little chicken on top. It is not a fancy place, but the wood paneling gives it a comfortable feel. Locals love it, and sometimes it gets crowded. At lunch, customers place orders at the counter; at supper, it is table service.

FROM I-40 AND I-240 Take Exit 53B to merge onto I-240 West/US 74 ALT West toward E. Asheville. Take Exit 5A for US 25/Merrimon Ave. Turn right onto US 25 North/Merrimon Ave. (passing by Bojangles). Luella's will be on the right.

Jeff Miller of Luella's Bar-B-Que in Asheville (photo by Mike Belleme)

AFTER EATING If you're in the mood for dessert, YoLo, which serves locally sourced frozen yogurt and toppings, is right across the parking lot. In the daytime, take a walk on the Weaver Park Trail that begins just around the corner.

Louise's Kitchen

115 Black Mountain Avenue, Black Mountain, NC 28711
(828) 357-5446
Monday–Saturday 7:30 A.M.–2:00 P.M.;
Sunday brunch 10:00 A.M.–2:00 P.M.
louisesblackmtn.com

Louise's is a favorite of Doug Orr, president emeritus of nearby Warren Wilson College and coauthor with Fiona Ritchie of *Wayfaring Strangers: The Musical Voyage from Scotland and Ulster to Appalachia*. Doug and his wife, Darcy, brag about the "wide variety of breakfast items (the blueberry waffles are a favorite) and lunch items such as Big Boy Burritos and Smoked Pork Quesadillas."

Twice a month at Louise's, Doug meets with "a little collection of retired doctors, college presidents, and Presbyterian ministers," and it is the place where Scotland's Fiona Ritchie, host of NPR's *Thistle and Shamrock*, eats when she visits the region for the annual Swannanoa Gathering of folk music performances and workshops.

The owners, Bud and Charissa Rainey, converted the white-framed building for restaurant use. Built in 1904 as private residence and known as the Stepp House, it is the oldest surviving building within the village of Black Mountain.

FROM I-40 Take Exit 64 onto Broadway toward Black Mountain. Go 0.5 mile. Turn left on Terry Estate Dr. and go 0.2 mile. Turn right on Black Mountain Ave. and go 0.2 mile. Louise's is on the right.

Countryside Barbeque

2070 Rutherford Road, Marion, NC 28752 · (828) 652-4885
Monday–Thursday 11:00 A.M.–8:00 P.M.;
Friday–Saturday 6:30 A.M.–9:00 P.M.; Sunday 11:00 A.M.–3:00 P.M.
countrysidebbq.net

If you're willing to weave around a few winding roads, there is a good payoff to be found at Countryside Barbecue. Tasty salads and sandwiches, including a good barbecue sandwich, a local favorite, are part of a diverse menu with daily specials and a Sunday buffet.

The side dishes, which they call "country sides" (collard greens, fried okra, sweet potatoes, and green beans), are prepared southern style. Get four of them on a vegetable plate for less than $7.

On Friday and Saturday mornings, you will find a crowd starting the day with a breakfast special of a country ham biscuit and baked cinnamon apples. Owners Rob Noyes and David Ditt are natives of Marion and have years of restaurant experience. They acquired the restaurant from longtime owners Gary and Lanetta Byrd in 2006. Countryside proudly reports that "President Obama and his team stopped by on their tour of North Carolina, and we were happy to provide them with the best of southern hospitality and catering!"

FROM I-40 Take Exit 86 (NC 226). From the intersection, head north on NC 226 toward Marion. Go 1 mile until NC 226 intersects with US 221. Turn right onto US 221 (Rutherford Rd.) and go about 0.5 mile. Countryside is on the left.

AFTER EATING Enjoy the small-town allure of the front porch in one of the "sit-and-chat" white rocking chairs. Or drive a few minutes to Fabulous Finds and Gifts at 290 E. Court St. to see if there is a treasure there for you. If you would like to walk away some of the good meal, the Peavine Trail begins nearby. Head north on Rutherford Rd. for about 0.5 mile to Ford Way. Turn right, and the trail begins on the left near the intersection with Glenwood Ave. This railroad corridor trail goes 1.5 miles to State St. in downtown Marion.

Asian Fusion Kitchen

402 W. Fleming Drive B, Morganton, NC 28655 · (828) 432-9092
Open every day 11:00 A.M.–9:00 P.M.

One thing I love about North Carolina is the way it's grown to welcome folks from all over the world, something that benefits us all in many ways. One of those ways is experiencing food you might never have tried in places you'd never expect to. For example, tucked away in an unassuming strip mall in the small foothills town of Morganton lies a wonderful story of hard work, welcoming community, and delicious Laotian cuisine. Dara Phrakousonh, chef and owner of Asian Fusion Kitchen, came to Morganton in the mid-1990s from the South Asian country of Laos and has been serving incredible food to lucky locals ever since. Since the restaurant opened in 2013, locals have been loving the sweet mango sticky rice, the spicy *larb*—a mix of ground meat and spices—and other dishes, including pineapple fried rice, served in an actual halved pineapple. There's no place like Asian Fusion Kitchen, and to find it in a small town like Morganton is a real treat.

Dara Phrakousonh left Laos to start a new life, bringing her love of food and people with her. Now her whole family lives in Morganton. In *Our State* magazine, Katy Clune writes that Dara is "known for her flavorful vegetables, and each morning she comes in at 9:00 A.M. to start the preparation, from scratch, of 25 gallons of seasoned chicken broth." That's dedication and, if I say so myself, great love going into cooking. Stop by Asian Fusion Kitchen to experience a little Laos in the foothills of North Carolina. And don't be afraid to ask for extra spice.

FROM I-40 Take Exit 103 to Burkemont Ave. and continue for about 1.5 miles before turning left onto Burkemont Ave. In less than 1 mile turn right onto W. Fleming Dr. Afterward turn left onto Coal Chute Rd. and immediately turn right and then left. Asian Fusion Kitchen will be on your right.

Asian Fusion Kitchen in Morganton (photo by Lucas Church)

··

Allison's Family Restaurant

1010 Burkemont Avenue, Morganton, NC 28655 · (828) 438-3662
Open every day 5:00 P.M.–10:00 P.M.

This longtime favorite in Morganton is just a few steps off the interstate. It's been more than 30 years since Jeff Allison struck out on
his own and became a business owner. First, he took over a Tastee-
Freez franchise and made it successful. Then he transformed it
into his own independent restaurant. Over the years it has become
home to a regular group of men who come for breakfast and gossip.
So breakfast is an important part of his business, with eggs, coffee,
biscuits, gravy, sausage, bacon, and livermush. (Yes, it's part of the
livermush belt extending from the Piedmont.)

 Lunch and dinner options include casual fare like barbecue,
hamburgers, and hot dogs, but leave room for a special something
from Jeff's Tastee-Freez days—a bountiful offering of homemade
ice cream, sundaes, and banana splits.

FROM I-40 Take Exit 103 toward Burkemont Ave. Turn left onto Burkemont Ave. and immediately turn left again, and Allison's will be on your left.

AFTER EATING Drive to downtown Morganton to visit the History Museum of Burke County at 201 W. Meeting St. Free admission. Call to check hours: (828) 437-1777. Hundreds of exhibits fill 10,000 sq. ft. of display space on two floors.

· ·

JD's Smokehouse

500 Malcolm Boulevard, Rutherford College, NC 28671
(across from the SECU) · (828) 522-1227
Thursday, Friday, and Saturday 11:00 A.M.–9:00 P.M.
jds-smokehouse.com

"This ain't your everyday BBQ. It's a weekend celebration!" is how the folks at JD's remind you that they are only open for 3 days— Thursday through Saturday. But they want you to know that if you stop on one of those 3 days, they will make your visit something special. When you go, try their signature sides, including cheese grits, sweet potato crunch, fried okra, jalapeño cheese grits, and Brunswick stew, in addition to their great barbecue.

The owners, Jim and Debbie Goare (hence JD's), have a playful sense of humor. In the women's restroom is a sign that says, "If you are smokin' in here you better be on fire!" Both Debbie and Jim grew up nearby in Burke County but were living in Georgia when they decided to open a restaurant. Not finding the right places in Georgia or South Carolina, Debbie says, "It was not my idea to go to Georgia in the first place, nor was it my idea to return to North Carolina. However, both moves, while a bit difficult in the beginning, have proven to be just what we needed." When they came back, they spent 2 years renovating a former manufacturing building, which they have turned into a cheerful and welcoming place for their customers.

The friendly staff at JD's Smokehouse

Oh, and I hope you like NASCAR, because JD's has racing memorabilia in troves. Jim's uncle, Robert Yates, the famed engine builder, NASCAR team owner, and Hall of Fame member, came to the restaurant's opening and helped Jim and Debbie acquire racing suits worn by Dale Jarrett, Ricky Rudd, and Elliott Sadler.

FROM I-40 Take Exit 113 toward Rutherford College/Connelly Springs. In less than 0.5 mile turn left onto Rutherford College Rd. Continue onto Malcolm Blvd., and in less than a mile JD's will be on your right.

AFTER EATING Drive through the town of Rutherford College, named after the college that merged into Brevard College in 1933, and search for remnants of the old college campus. Ask Debbie for directions to the Town Hall, where there is more information about the history of the town and the college. Or drive to nearby Valdese, with its memory walks and museums honoring the Waldensian settlers.

Randy's BBQ, another eatery in the area,
is described in the I-77 chapter.

. . . .

Keaton's BBQ

17365 Cool Springs Road, Cleveland, NC 27013 · (704) 278-1619
11:00 A.M.–2:00 P.M. and 5:00 P.M.–8:00 P.M. daily
MAY NOT ACCEPT CREDIT CARDS
keatonsoriginalbbq.com

I don't know how to say it other than this: Keaton's is something different—something you should not miss.

First of all, you have to drive around in the country for about 3 miles from the interstate intersection to get to Keaton's. But when you find it, there is nothing but Keaton's anywhere around. In other words, everybody who goes to Keaton's is simply going to Keaton's. They do not just "happen by."

Second, if you try the house specialty, fried barbecued chicken, you are going to have a delightful taste experience unlike anything you have ever had before. First it's crispy fried, then dipped in Keaton's special sauce that blends with the crust and seeps into the meat.

Third, at Keaton's, things are done "their way." For instance, when I entered the cinderblock building and lined up behind the counter, I looked up at the menu on the wall. It told me that my order of fried barbecued chicken would come with a slice of white bread and nothing else. To get one of their side dishes, I would have to order and pay for it separately. When I ordered iced tea, they gave me a tray with a glass of tea and a pitcher to take to my seat. They gave me a number that was my table or booth assignment.

I paid in cash, went to my assigned seat, and waited for an attendant to bring my fried barbecued chicken.

Keaton's is open when it wants to be—only 4 days a week, Wednesday through Saturday. So why, then, you ask, is Keaton's so popular? Why does it have a loyal following of locals—and out-of-towners who travel great distances to gather there? It is the special fried barbecued chicken dish, of course. Oh, boy, does it taste good. It is also the wonderful variety of people who work and eat there.

Then, too, there is the history. Local customer Jerry Cartner told me that he has been eating chicken and other dishes regularly at Keaton's for more than 30 years. In the old days, it was even more different, he said.

B. W. Keaton, who founded Keaton's around 1953, came from a nearby family of African American farmers. In the early days, according to Cartner, Keaton's was a very small building with a dirt floor. Locals dropped by to get Mr. Keaton's chicken and drink a beer. If anybody started to get rowdy, Mr. Keaton could keep things under control—everybody knew that he kept a shotgun under the counter.

"Keaton had a brother who always took the orders," Cartner said. "He never wrote any of them down and remembered everything perfectly. We tried to trick him by making the orders complicated, but we never could fool him." Keaton died in 1989. His niece, Kathleen Murray, and her son, David Dwayne Harris, run Keaton's now. The shotgun is gone, and the crowd is family oriented and very orderly. Still, it is one of the few "home-cooking" places near the interstate where you can get a beer with your meal.

The clientele is decidedly mixed. On one of my visits, I met two sophisticated women decorators who now live in Toronto and Chicago. They were visiting their mother, who lives in Winston-Salem. "Don't use our names, but we bring our mother to Keaton's every time we come home." "How long does it take you all to get here from Winston-Salem?" I asked them. "Oh, that depends on how hungry we are," they said, laughing. "And we used to know some people who came down here regularly in a chauffeured Rolls-Royce. They would bring their silverware and cloth napkins with them."

If you find your way to Keaton's today, you'll likely see a parking lot crowded with pickup trucks rather than Rolls-Royces. But there may be a Lexus or two, which is good evidence that Keaton's special fried barbecued chicken still has fans from every station in life.

FROM I-40 Take Exit 162 (US 64 West). Follow US 64, heading west for about 1.5 miles to its intersection with Woodleaf Rd. You will see a Keaton's sign on the corner to the left. Turn left onto Woodleaf Rd. and follow it through rolling countryside for about 1.5 miles until you see Keaton's on the right. (Woodleaf Rd. changes into Cool Springs Rd. when you leave Iredell County and go into Rowan County about 0.5 mile before you reach Keaton's.)

AFTER EATING How about a quick trip to Pittsburg? Follow Cool Springs Rd. about 0.5 mile, and where it intersects with Chenault/Steel/Dooley Rd. is a crossroads that Google Maps identifies as Pittsburg. Nothing is there other than a very nice church building. Warning: There is no mention of Pittsburg, North Carolina, in William Powell's *North Carolina Gazetteer*. But you can still say you have been there.

. . . .

Miller's Restaurant

710 Wilkesboro Street, Mocksville, NC 27028 · (336) 751-2621
Monday–Thursday 5:00 A.M.–10:00 P.M.;
Friday 6:00 A.M.–11:00 P.M.;
Saturday 6:00 A.M.–9:00 P.M.; Sunday 7:00 A.M.–10:00 P.M.
millersrestaurant52.com

On the outside, Miller's Restaurant still looks like the same truck stop that Sheek Miller founded back in 1952 at the busy intersection of Highways 64 and 601. Although it's now a little bit off the beaten path, a few old truckers and some smart new ones still find their way to Miller's. But today it is more a community and family gathering place for folks in Mocksville.

On the inside, visitors from the 1950s would feel right at home. They could still sit at the same counter or choose a table in the dining room that has not changed much in 50 years. When I stopped for supper, the dining room was crowded with young families, retired couples, one or two truckers, and a few folks like me who came to eat alone. Friendly waitresses dressed in T-shirts and shorts kept busy serving us all. My waitress was a Miller cousin, and she told me that most of her coworkers had been there for "a long, long time." Sheek Miller would be proud of his son, Kip, the current owner. Kip runs the place the same way his dad did back in 1953.

I asked a woman who was eating there with her husband and three children why they came to Miller's. "We like it because we can get something for all of us here," she replied. "One of the kids had breakfast. Another had a meat-and-two-vegetables plate, and the rest of us had seafood. And it is all good."

Hungry for vegetables, I ordered fried squash, baked apples, and creamed potatoes. The vegetables tasted fresh and delicious. The round, crisp hushpuppies that came with them were good enough to compete with those at North Carolina's best barbecue restaurants. My waitress kept my iced tea glass full and gave me a big smile every time she passed by.

When she finally brought me a bill, I realized that I had filled myself up for just a few dollars. Even if the prices were not so reasonable and the food so good, I would be coming back to Miller's whenever I could, if only to take a trip back to the 1950s.

FROM I-40 Take Exit 170 (US 601/Mocksville). Follow US 601 for 1.5 miles. At a stoplight at the intersection with Wilkesboro St., turn left and go one block.

AFTER EATING Visit Joppa Cemetery, about 0.6 mile north on Yadkinville Rd., on the right. Daniel Boone's parents, Squire and Sarah Boone, are buried there.

Deano's Barbecue

140 N. Clement Street, Mocksville, NC 27028 · (336) 751-5820
Tuesday–Saturday 11:00 A.M.–8:00 P.M.; closed Sunday–Monday

Owner Dean Allen has been in the barbecue business since 1961. As a high school student, he worked as a curb boy for Buck's Barbecue restaurant, which he later bought and renamed Deano's. His long experience brings good results that have been praised by Jim Early, author of *The Best Tar Heel Barbecue: Manteo to Murphy*, who says Deano's barbecue is "pound-the-table good."

Early says that the brown pieces mixed in the chopped meat "give each bite that pungent smoky taste that makes the flavor explode in your mouth." He continues, lyrically, that the sliced white meat from the shoulder of the pig "is moist, tender and melts in your mouth. When it holds hands with the sauce, they dance!"

All that, plus the crowds of locals who visit at mealtimes, definitely makes a visit to Deano's worth the short trip into downtown Mocksville.

FROM I-40 Take Exit 170 (US 601/Mocksville). Follow US 601 for 1.5 miles. At a stoplight at the intersection with Wilkesboro St., turn left and go 0.7 mile. Turn left at Gaither and then immediately turn right at N. Clement St.

La Botana Home Made Mexican Food

1547 Hanes Mall Boulevard, Winston-Salem, NC 27113
Monday–Thursday 11:00 A.M.–8:30 P.M.;
Friday 11:00 A.M.–9:00 P.M.; Saturday 11:00 A.M.–9:00 P.M.;
closed Sunday

Step inside this busy cantina and you'll be greeted by the delicious smells of real Mexican cooking—their name even says "Home Made"—but you'll also find friendly faces. Nestled in a small shopping plaza just off Hanes Mall Boulevard, La Botana, which roughly means "snack" in Spanish, might not look like much from the outside, but it's what's inside that counts.

You'll be greeted at the door by a sign announcing "things you should know before you enter." One of those things is they do not serve fancy food or fancy drinks. They're right. They serve good, home-cooked food that is worth the short trip through Winston-Salem traffic to get.

What makes La Botana special, you ask? After all, there are a lot of good Mexican restaurants just a hop and a skip off our state roadways. Well, I'll tell you. The folks at La Botana like to keep you on your toes. They change their menu on a regular basis and feature food you won't usually find in a typical Mexican restaurant, including lamb, asparagus, and tofu. The *Winston-Salem Journal* raves about the *molcajete*, a traditional stew served in a piping-hot stone bowl. Mary Haglund, head chef of Mary's Gourmet Diner in Winston-Salem, loves their authentically cooked beans and veggies—high praise, indeed.

Now, don't get me wrong: you'll also find all the tacos, burritos, and enchiladas you'd expect, all wonderfully prepared. La Botana has been voted best Winston-Salem Mexican restaurant 4 years running, so they know a thing or two about pleasing people.

But what makes La Botana really special? It's the people. From the family who runs the restaurant to the local customers who religiously gather to enjoy the food, it's the people that make La Botana a true standout and worth finding. Go on a Sunday and you'll see folks from all walks of life in their church clothes, enjoying fried steak *tortas* (Mexican-style sandwiches), quesadillas, and more. Go for lunch or dinner on a weekday and listen to the conversations in English and Spanish, all while soccer matches play on the televisions overhead.

A short trip just off I-40, friendly faces and delicious food await you at La Botana. Just don't fill up on the savory chips and salsa!

FROM I-40 Take Exit 188 from I-40 and merge onto US 421 toward Yadkinville/Wilkesboro. About a mile down the road, take Exit 239 for Jonestown Rd. Take a left onto Jonestown, and in less than 0.25 mile, you will turn left onto Hanes Mall Blvd. La Botana is 0.25 mile down Hanes Mall Blvd. in a small shopping center.

AFTER EATING Hanes Mall is right next door.

....

Real Q

4885 Country Club Road, Winston-Salem, NC 27104
(336) 760-3457
Monday–Saturday 11:00 A.M.–10:00 P.M.; closed Sunday

When my Davidson College classmate Dr. Gene Adcock told me that the barbecue at Real Q, formerly Little Richard's, was Lexington style and the best in Winston-Salem, I knew I would have to try it out. I was not disappointed.

Richard Berrier, the owner and operator, grew up in Davidson County and learned the art of wood-fired barbecue cooking from Leroy McCarn at the Country Kitchen in Midway. While he was in high school and college, he worked first at curb service, then the cash register, and later in the kitchen, learning every aspect of cooking and providing homelike service. After Richard finished his studies at Appalachian State, Mr. McCarn offered him the chance to run his business, which he did from 1985 until about 1990. In April 1991, after deciding to go out on his own, he opened what is now Real Q and has been there ever since.

The inside of Real Q takes you back about 60 years, with the jukebox playing songs from the 1950s and 1960s. The walls are decorated with old signs that Berrier has collected through the years. He says people bring in old signs for him to display. "That old Coca-Cola clock is probably worth $500 at the flea market," he told me, "but one of my friends brought it here to display, just so other people could see it."

"I'm the only one still cooking with all wood in Winston-Salem," he says. The aroma of the wood cooking adds to the experience. Berrier cooks only the pig's shoulders, making for a clean, delicious, Lexington-style offering. The food is great, but the charm of Real Q is its diverse clientele, ranging from judges to ditchdiggers. Berrier says, "The construction workers feel just as comfortable as the judges, because we make them know that they can walk in here with their muddy shoes and feel right at home." And feel right at home I did too, knowing that the next time I'm headed toward the mountains on I-40, Real Q will provide an oasis of old-time home cooking just a few miles from the interstate.

FROM I-40 Take Exit 188 to merge onto US 421 north toward Yadkinville/Wilkesboro. Continue straight for 1 mile and take Exit 238. Make a right onto Jonestown Rd. Continue for 0.5 miles on Jonestown Rd., then turn left onto Country Club Rd. Continue for 0.5 miles. Real Q will be on your right.

The Diner

108 N. Gordon Drive, Winston-Salem, NC 27104 · (336) 765-9158
Monday–Friday 5:30 A.M.–2:00 P.M.;
Saturday 6:00 A.M.–12:00 P.M.; closed Sunday

According Gene Adcock, who introduced me to The Diner, there is good news and bad news. First, the bad news: Steve Eaton Jr., whose grandfather opened the diner in 1968, recently sold the business.

The good news is that the new owners are doing a good job. Gene wrote, "We still go on occasion; many of our former neighborhood friends continue as regulars. Importantly, the food is still good, especially breakfast. The head cook, Poncho, and his family bought the business when Steve decided to retire. They redecorated the place, so that it is much 'fresher' looking but, of course, were smart to keep the food and family-customer ambiance the same. The success of The Diner continues under new management."

The change in ownership made me remember when I fell in love with The Diner on my first visit. "God bless you!" the cashier told a departing customer as I walked in for breakfast one early morning.

My waitress, Stephanie, persuaded me to try the breaded tenderloin with a scrambled eggs plate. It was delicious. When Steve stopped by my table, he explained that, while the breaded tenderloin is a mainstay at The Diner, the most popular item is the black skillet pan gravy, which is served as a separate dish.

Steve told me about his family's long history in the restaurant business in Winston-Salem. His grandfather Raymond Eaton opened The Diner about 1968 in a nearby building. Raymond learned the cooking trade in the navy and then worked at the old Zinzendorf Hotel in downtown Winston-Salem, leaving that job to open the Main Street Luncheonette, located where the Forsyth County courthouse sits today. With the proceeds from the sale of the luncheonette, Raymond Eaton bought a small existing restaurant with about nine stools and a counter, paying about $300. Over the years the business expanded. About 1979 Raymond sold the business to his son, Steve's dad. He moved it to its current location and expanded it to about 100 seats. In 1996, his dad sold The Diner to Steve. Just a few months later, Steve's dad passed away. For a long time Raymond's widow, Rosemary Eaton, came in to make desserts like the banana pudding, cobbler, and pies that are favorites at lunchtime. My waitress, Stephanie Eaton, was Steve's daughter and Rosemary's great-granddaughter.

I asked Steve how this small restaurant could have prospered over four generations of the family. He explained, "There is nothing prim and proper about us. You either like us or you don't. But most people like us. They enjoy picking at me—and I at them. You get to know them by their first names and learn about what is going on in their lives."

"It is sort of like *Cheers*, the old TV program, isn't it?" I asked. "That is about it," Steve replied.

So far the new owners and their families are doing well, but it will take them a long time to catch up with the four generations of Eatons who put their mark on this little *Cheers*-like gathering place.

FROM I-40 At Exit 188 (intersection of I-40, I-40 Business, and US 421) take US 421 West (toward Yadkinville and Wilkesboro). Follow US 421 West for about 0.5 mile. Take the first exit (Exit 239, Jonestown Rd.). At the end of the ramp turn right and head north on Jonestown Rd. Follow Jonestown Rd. for about 0.5 mile until it dead-ends into Country Club Rd. Turn right on Country Club Rd. and go about 1 mile until you reach the intersection of N. Gordon Dr. Turn left on N. Gordon Dr. and you will see The Diner on the left.

AFTER EATING Walk around the corner to Country Club Rd. and visit the Train Loft model shop or the House of Cards game store.

Sweet Potatoes

607 N. Trade Street N.W., Winston-Salem, NC 27101
(336) 727-4844
Tuesday–Thursday 11:00 A.M.–10:00 P.M.;
Friday–Saturday 11:00 A.M.–10:00 P.M.;
Sunday brunch 10:30 A.M.–3:00 P.M.; closed Monday
sweetpotatoes.ws

In 2003, Stephanie Tyson and Vivián Joiner opened Sweet Potatoes Restaurant in Winston-Salem's Downtown Arts District and took the city by storm with their combination of soul food, elegant presentation, and smart marketing. They call their fare "unique, southern inspired" and "uptown, down-home cooking."

Chef Tyson, a North Carolina native, says that she has infused her southern upbringing into the soul of her restaurant. Joiner brings years of restaurant management to the team.

Fried chicken, fried green tomatoes, okra, and other soul food items draw regular customers and visitors from all walks of life. But even in this historic tobacco town, the sweet potato is king here. The pies, muffins, biscuits, and fries all come from North Carolina's new favorite crop.

Lots of business work gets done here. The *Winston-Salem Journal's* former editorial page editor, John Railey, gives Sweet Potatoes credit for giving him a place to work on his book *Rage to Redemption in the Sterilization Age.*

FROM I-40 From I-40 Business take Exit 5D for Main St. toward downtown/1st St. Turn right onto S. Main St. and go 0.7 mile. Then turn left onto W. 6th St. Turn right at the second cross street onto Trade St. N.W. Sweet Potatoes will be on the right.

AFTER EATING Walk to the corner of Trade and Fifth, where the 100-plus-year-old former U.S. Post Office and Courthouse still stands and has been transformed into the Millennium Center for

Happy visitors to Sweet Potatoes

use for special events. Oprah Winfrey rented the building to host Maya Angelou's 85th birthday gala. At the party, according to Millennium owner Greg Carlyle, Angelou drank a bottle of Johnnie Walker Blue Label with him.

Plaza Restaurant

806 NC 66, Kernersville, NC 27284 · (336) 996-7923
Monday–Friday 10:30 A.M.–8:30 P.M.;
Saturday 7:30 A.M.–8:30 P.M.; Sunday 9:30 A.M.–2:00 P.M.
plaza-restaurant.com

On my search for the best home-cooking places near the interstate, I usually avoid restaurants in shopping centers. I look for family-owned places that have been around a long time. Usually I find them in old, freestanding buildings. These are the places that local people have come to know for their good food and fellowship, rather than for extravagant surroundings designed to attract travelers and other passers-by.

But there are exceptions. So when my friends at the *Kernersville News*, the local newspaper, told me that folks gathered at Plaza Restaurant for good country cooking, I decided to give it a try, even though it sits right in the middle of a shopping center. The restaurant was spiffy clean, and at lunchtime the day I visited, it was completely full. When I tasted my plate of fresh vegetables, I understood why.

When Alex Kroustalis bought Plaza in 1995, he gathered a group of experts to make suggestions about what changes he should make. After due deliberation, they told him, "Change nothing but the lock on the door." Alex followed that suggestion. He attributed his success to four things: "A clean place, good food, reasonable prices, and service. Everything else will take care of itself."

Stephen Kroustalis acquired Plaza from his uncle Alex in 2007. Stephen serves a different set of specials every day, always with a big selection of meats and fresh vegetables. Undoubtedly, one of the secrets to the Plaza Restaurant's success is variety.

Although Stephen has made some extensive changes, including a complete renovation and revamping of the menu, he says he still follows those same old guidelines.

FROM I-40 Take Exit 203 (NC 66/Kernersville). Head north on NC 66 for 2 miles. The Plaza Restaurant is on the left in the Plaza 66 Shopping Center.

....

Prissy Polly's BBQ

729 NC 66, Kernersville, NC 27284 · (336) 993-5045
Monday–Saturday 11:00 A.M.–8:00 P.M.; closed Sunday
prissypollys.com

The judge looked at me with puzzled disdain when he learned that I had omitted this restaurant from an earlier book. "How could you miss Prissy Polly's?" asked the late Judge Dickson Phillips, former dean of the UNC School of Law and U.S. Court of Appeals judge. "It's one of our favorite places—some of the best barbecue I have ever had." Lots of people agree, and they sometimes line up outside, knowing they can choose either Lexington- or Eastern-style North Carolina barbecue when they get inside.

When Loran Whaley opened up in 1991 and named his new restaurant after his mother, Pauline, whose nickname was "Prissy Polly," he served Eastern-style barbecue exclusively. But when his sons Greg and Gary noticed that many of their customers were covering their plates with a tomato-based sauce, they determined to add a bit of Lexington to the menu. "It has worked out well for us. And the customers like the option," Greg says.

He emphasizes the variety of menu options, including "Cracker Meal Catfish, Low Country Shrimp, Baby Back Spare Ribs, Large Dinner Salads, Fried Chicken, Boneless BBQ Chicken, Chicken Tenders, and Brunswick Stew." After taking a breath, he says, "We still offer an array of sides like fried okra, black-eyed peas, barbecued [grilled] potatoes, country green beans, and our now famous loaded potato salad. Desserts include comforting banana pudding, southern pecan pie, key lime pie, apple crisp, and chocolate cobbler."

Greg asserts that they are "still serving the best hushpuppies in the state and award-winning sweet ice tea." And finally, he brags,

"The word has spread far and wide, that heading west of Raleigh-Durham we are the last bastion of Eastern NC–style barbecue."

FROM I-40 Take Exit 203 (NC 66/Kernersville). Head north on NC 66 for 2 miles. Prissy Polly's is on the left across from the Plaza 66 Shopping Center.

AFTER EATING Drive to downtown Kernersville to get a look at the famous Körner's Folly, a historic and eccentric three-and-a-half story brick dwelling with a shingled, cross-gable roof located at 413 S. Main St.

Another eatery in the vicinity, Soprano's Italian Restaurant,
is described in the I-73/74 chapter, and Kepley's Bar-B-Q,
described in the I-85 chapter, is also not too far away.

. . . .

Stamey's Barbecue

2206 W. Gate City Boulevard, Greensboro, NC 27403
(336) 299-9888
Monday–Saturday 10:00 A.M.–9:00 P.M.; closed Sunday
stameys.com

No list of home-cooking spots near I-40 would be complete without a salute to this legendary place.

Three generations of Stameys have made their barbecue business one of the most famous and most successful in the state. Stamey's still holds to its tradition of cooking pork shoulders over wood coals. Even if the barbecue was not so good, I would stop just to order a bowl of their peach cobbler, with its flaky, buttery pastry over juicy peaches surrounded by rich, sweet sauce.

But it's the barbecue and side dishes that draw the most people, from Greensboro and all over the state. I saw several teams of construction workers in baseball caps eating at tables next to high-powered women wearing stylish silk scarves. The high ceilings and bright interiors make this restaurant a cheerful place that everybody traveling with you will enjoy.

The founder of the business, Warner Stamey, was born in 1911 and began cooking barbecue when he was in high school. After operating eateries in Lexington, Warner opened his first Greensboro location in 1953. His sons Charles and Keith took over the business and opened the current location in 1979. Keith passed away in 2000. Charles's son, Chip, is the current owner, while Charles, though retired, serves as "pitmaster emeritus."

Stamey's takes pride in the cooking methods that Warner learned as a boy: "We still slow cook our barbecue over a pit of hardwood hickory coals. The brick pits are completely enclosed, except for a bit of breathing room at the bottom. The hardwood coals are carefully monitored because they will dry the face of the pork if they get too hot. As each 15-pound pork shoulder cooks, the drippings fall onto the hot coals, sending the hickory smoke flavor into the pork."

Stamey's is a regular stopping point for campaigning politicians of both parties. Donald Trump paid a visit during the 2016 campaign.

FROM I-40 Take Exit 217 off I-40. Head north on W. Gate City Blvd. Go about 1 mile (noting the signs directing you to the Coliseum). Stamey's is on the left, directly across W. Gate City Blvd. from the Coliseum.

AFTER EATING Visit the grounds of the massive Greensboro Coliseum just across the street.

*Other eateries in the area are described in the I-85 chapter,
including Jack's Barbecue, Hursey's Pig-Pickin' Bar-B-Q,
Village Diner, and the Hillsborough BBQ Company.*

Zack's Hot Dogs

201 W. Davis Street, Burlington, NC 27215 · (336) 226-4746
Monday–Thursday 6:30 A.M.–9:00 P.M.;
Friday–Saturday 6:30 A.M.–10:00 P.M.; closed Sunday
zackshotdogs.com

If you're on the interstate and have a hankering for a good hot dog, I got you covered. But don't take my word for it—go ahead and ask any Burlingtonian where the best dogs in town are, and the unanimous response that you'll get is Zack's Hot Dogs. Established in 1929 and still family owned to this day, Zack's is an institution that serves great food and fast service on a dime. Founder Zack Touloupas migrated to the United States from Greece in the early 1900s, eventually settling in Burlington. He soon opened the Alamance Hot Wienie Lunch restaurant, which became Zack's Hot Dogs.

Zack's grandson, also named Zack, runs the restaurant, which is located in downtown Burlington, about 10 minutes from Interstate 40. As soon as you step inside, you are immediately struck with the no-frills character of the place. But don't let that fool you. Advance to the counter and order breakfast, lunch, or dinner and you will be struck with the quickness of service and the tastiness of the food. Locals are always packed into Zack's, especially around lunchtime. Order a cheese dog, a block of cheese on a hot dog bun with toppings of your choice, or a combo dog, a hot dog with mustard, slaw, and onions; and don't forget to add Zack's own secret chili recipe—something the founder concocted himself and is a big part of why Zack's has lasted nearly a century.

Zack recently told the *Burlington Times News* that "we have tried to change every once in a while, but my philosophy is do one or two things, do them real well and you don't have to worry." With that kind of philosophy behind the counter, how can you go wrong?

FROM I-40 Take Exit 143 for NC 62 toward Burlington Downtown/ Alamance. After about 3 miles, turn left onto NC 62 North/Alamance Rd. In a little over a mile turn slightly right onto S. Church Rd. After about 1.5 miles turn right onto W. Davis St., and Zack's will be on the left.

....

Sunrise Biscuit Kitchen

1305 E. Franklin Street, Chapel Hill, NC 27514 · (919) 933-1324
Monday–Saturday 6:00 A.M.–2:30 P.M.;
Sunday 7:00 A.M.–2:30 P.M.

There are few places as beloved in Chapel Hill as Sunrise Biscuit Kitchen. Nearly every day you'll find cars in line for the drive-through (this particular Sunrise is drive-through only!) backed out onto Franklin Street—it's that popular. Buttery biscuits, fresh sweet iced tea, hot and crispy hashbrowns: that's what I call a satisfying breakfast. Not a lot of folks know that Sunrise has two locations, and the one in Chapel Hill is not the original restaurant. Sunrise was originally started in the small town of Louisburg, North Carolina, by David Allen, and Allen based Sunrise's biscuit recipe on his grandmother's. If that isn't family cooking, I don't know what is.

Even if you're not from North Carolina, you might recognize Sunrise from appearances on the Food Network, the Travel Channel, NPR's *The Splendid Table*, and even in the film *Bad Grandpa*, which inspired its own fried chicken, bacon, egg, and cheese biscuit.

But don't skip this Chapel Hill institution if you're hankering for lunch, not breakfast. Sunrise offers southern staples like barbecue, chicken salad, and hot dogs, too. While there isn't indoor seating at this location, you can still park your car and watch as Chapel Hillians gather to celebrate maybe the best southern food, the humble biscuit.

FROM I-40 Take Exit 270 for 15-501 South and go about 3 miles. Sunrise will be on your right.

AFTER EATING You're just a few minutes from the beautiful UNC–Chapel Hill campus. Take a moment to visit the Coker Arboretum, a free botanical garden, open year-round, on E. Cameron Ave. with hundreds of native and exotic flora. Dogs are allowed, so Fido can stretch his legs while you burn off those biscuit calories.

Other eateries in the area are described in the I-85 chapter, including Bennett Pointe Grill & Bar and Bullock's Bar-B-Cue.

Sutton's Drug Store

159 E. Franklin Street, Chapel Hill, NC 27514 · (919) 942-5161
Monday–Friday 7:00 A.M.–6:30 P.M.;
Saturday 7:00 A.M.–4:30 P.M.; Sunday 9:00 A.M.–3:00 P.M.
suttonsdrugstore.com/menu

"Why isn't Sutton's in your book? Every time I stop by, you are there!"

I got this a lot from folks who read the first edition of *Roadside Eateries*, and yes, it's true that I am a regular at Sutton's, especially at breakfast. It has come to be something like my second home, my gathering place.

If I am not that hungry, Marta is happy to bring me a cup of coffee and a couple of biscuits. She also brings me the special jar of Sutton's jam that I buy and Sutton's keeps for me in the small refrigerator in the back. But if I *am* hungry, I go for the Number 3 with eggs over easy, grits, biscuits, and a boatload of bacon all for about $6. You can't beat the flavor or the price.

At lunchtime, Sutton's famous hamburgers are almost everybody's favorite—including mine.

Although the food is great, owner Don Pinney and former owner and current consultant John Woodard will tell you it's sense of community that's drawn people to Sutton's since it first opened in 1923.

Police officers, fire officers, and maintenance workers mingle with Tar Heel basketball players. Lennie Rosenbluth, star of the 1957 championship team, often stops by on Fridays. Sheriff Charles

Sutton's Drug Store in Chapel Hill (photo by Lucas Church)

Blackwood and Judge Joe Butner consult with attorney Bob Epting about their cases for the day.

Don Pinney says his tight group of servers and cooks, Marta, Holly, Elsa, Demos, and others, are key to his and Sutton's success. They make me happy every time I visit.

FROM I-40 Take Exit 266 to merge onto NC 86 South/Martin Luther King Jr. Blvd. toward Chapel Hill. Follow that road for about 4.5 miles to the intersection with Franklin St. Turn left onto E. Franklin St. Sutton's will be on your left.

AFTER EATING Walk a block to the post office and admire the mural celebrating the laying of the cornerstone for the first building at UNC.

Allen & Son Bar-B-Que

5650 US 15-501, Pittsboro, NC 27312 · (919) 542-2294
Monday–Saturday 11:00 A.M.–8:00 P.M.; closed Sunday
stubbsandsonbbq.com

Allen & Son near I-40 and I-85 north of Chapel Hill shut its doors in early 2019. For many years, owner Keith Allen worked early and late to chop the hickory wood and manage the slow-cooked fire that brings pork shoulders to perfect eating condition. *Southern Living* praised Allen & Son and made it one of its "Top Picks" in southern barbecue joints.

Keith Allen's sudden departure from the barbecue scene left us gasping and wondering where we could go for the same kind of good barbecue that Keith gave us. Some fans are going to another Allen & Son a few miles south of Chapel Hill, about halfway to Pittsboro. And for a hungry traveler, the detour to the other Allen & Son might be a very good option. In fact, my friends in Pittsboro, Governors' Club, Carolina Meadows, and Fearrington swear by "their" Allen & Son.

It shared a name with the more famous barbecue north of Chapel Hill and the question always arises: what is the connection?

The same family started both places. Keith Allen told me his family still owns the Pittsboro location. But Jimmy Stubbs, who also owns Stubbs & Son BBQ with locations in Sanford and Carthage, has run the Pittsboro Allen & Son for 20 years. Stubbs says he is also the owner. I think both are telling the truth—the Allens still own the Pittsboro building in which Stubbs owns and runs the restaurant.

Although Keith cooked with wood coals, Jimmy does what most other barbecue eateries do these days: he uses gas to prepare his Eastern-style North Carolina chopped barbecue. Only the most traditional minded of the 'cue tribe would argue that Jimmy's is not real barbecue—and even they will admit that Jimmy's results are mighty tasty. Jimmy also brags about his homemade coleslaw, which he says is "second to none." He continues, "It has a sweet and slightly spicy flavor that adds the perfect taste and texture to not only the barbecue but also the burgers, hot dogs, or as a side dish. It's made fresh every morning at Stubbs & Son."

One visitor who blended the pork with the vinegar-based sauce and the slaw declared the result to be "culinary harmony."

FROM I-40 Take Exit 273. Follow US 15-501 toward Pittsboro for about 17 miles. Allen & Son will be on the left.

AFTER EATING Now that you are close, don't miss the chance to visit downtown Pittsboro, a small town that has revived and come alive. For instance, French Connections at 178 Hillsboro St. has both a store and a front yard full of an eclectic variety of fabrics, antiques, table linens, art, and crafts from far-flung places like France and Mexico.

. . . .

The Chicken Hut

3019 Fayetteville Street, Durham, NC 27707 · (919) 682-5697
Monday–Friday 11:30 A.M.–3:30 P.M.;
closed Saturday and Sunday

This unassuming little gem in Durham has a long history. Established originally in 1957 by the late Peggy and Claiborne Tapp III as the Chicken Box, the Chicken Hut claims to be the second-oldest continually operating restaurant in Durham. The restaurant is now run by their son, Tre Tapp, and is staffed by relatives. I think Tre and his family have clearly learned a thing or two over the years about making good, comforting home-cooked food.

Friendly faces abound at the Chicken Hut, along with some of the best fried chicken in the state and mac and cheese that will knock your socks off. Make sure to check the website before you visit; the Chicken Hut has a rotating list of daily specials, from baked spaghetti and oxtails to chitterlings and fried shrimp—and the shrimp is fresh, crunchy, and delicious, paired expertly with their tangy coleslaw. But don't worry: that fried chicken is served every day.

Also, the Tapps care about their community. During the early days of the COVID-19 pandemic, the Chicken Hut partnered with a local school to provide free hot meals to kids who needed breakfast and lunch, ultimately feeding close to a thousand young people in Durham. I know a lot of folks say they show their love with food, and it's clear that the Tapps have a lot of love for their community.

FROM I-40 Take Exit 279 for US 15-501 North and continue for 2 miles. Follow signs for 15-501 Business, then in 2 miles turn right onto Legion Ave., followed by a left onto W. Cornwallis Rd. Go approximately 1.7 miles, then take a left onto Fayetteville St. and continue for 0.25 mile. The Chicken Hut will be on your right.

AFTER EATING The Chicken Hut is close to the North Carolina Central University campus, one of the most renowned historically Black colleges in the country. Take a walk on the grounds or head west to visit the natural beauty of Duke Forest.

. . . .

Saltbox Seafood Joint

2637 Durham–Chapel Hill Boulevard, Durham, NC 27707
(919) 237-3499
Tuesday–Saturday 11:00 A.M.–6:00 P.M. (or until
the fish runs out); closed Sunday–Monday
ORIGINAL LOCATION:
608 N. Mangum Street, Durham, NC 27701 · (919) 908-8970
Tuesday–Saturday 11:00 A.M.–6:00 P.M. (or until
the fish runs out); closed Sunday–Monday
saltboxseafoodjoint.com

Since the last edition of *Roadside Eateries*, Saltbox chef Ricky Moore has been just a little busy. He opened a new Saltbox Seafood Joint in south Durham, wrote a cookbook—the *Saltbox Seafood Joint Cookbook*, which I recommend you go out and get right now—and

Ricky Moore of Saltbox Seafood in Durham (photo by Baxter Miller)

has been featured in *Garden & Gun*, *Southern Living*, and *Our State*, among many other fine publications. Though he's a busy man, don't worry—he's still at it, cooking incredible food for lucky locals.

This new Saltbox is a major change from the original location. Now you can sit down with that mess of fried shrimp and enjoy some nice air-conditioning in the summer months. And even though the food is first-rate, the nautical-themed décor is another good reason to stop by.

Now, Ricky's success isn't the least surprising. He's been in the food business all his life. He grew up catching and cooking fish in Eastern North Carolina. He cooked during his 7 years in the army, studied at the Culinary Institute of America, and worked at the fine

Glasshalfull restaurant in Carrboro and as the opening executive chef at Georgio's in Cary.

On the menu at the second location is the seafood Ricky's famous for: shrimp, salmon, trout, monkfish, catfish, soft-shell crab, tuna, and more. Keep in mind that whatever seafood is listed on that chalkboard, it's all freshly caught. Moore explained to me that it's not easy or cheap to get the best fish. He has to take into account that "the value is in the quality of fresh product we provide. Good, fresh seafood is not cheap, and the North Carolina fishermen deserve to get top dollar for their catch."

Back in the day, *Saveur* raved about Ricky's food, saying, "The preparations reveal chef Ricky Moore's creativity and skill: toothsome grilled bluefish in a smoky-spicy rub of paprika and Aleppo pepper; an oyster roll, the plump, sweet mollusks dusted in fine cornmeal before frying, then topped with a fresh herb-laced slaw." They're right, of course, but they didn't mention the Hush-Honeys, Ricky's version of the hushpuppy. They're a little salty, a little spicy, and a little sweet. They're the perfect complement to the best seafood you're liable to find anywhere, let alone in the middle of the Tar Heel State.

FROM I-40 *If headed east*: Take Exit 270 for US 15-501 North/Durham–Chapel Hill Blvd. and turn left toward Durham. In about 1.5 miles, keep to the left and stay on Durham–Chapel Hill Blvd. Continue on Durham–Chapel Hill Blvd. for about 2.5 miles. The Saltbox Seafood Joint will be on the right.

If headed west: Take Exit 270, but turn right toward Durham and follow the above directions.

AFTER EATING Go get some wonderful pastries from Guglhupf, just down the street, and then go walk it off at the nearby Rockwood Park.

Neomonde Mediterranean Café/Market

3817 Beryl Road, Raleigh, NC 27607 · (919) 828-1628
Monday–Sunday 10:00 A.M.–9:00 P.M.
neomonde.com

When former state legislator Phillip Baddour was chair of the state's Clean Water Management Trust Fund, he asked me to serve as interim director. While we were working closely together, he taught me a lot about the background of his and other North Carolina families with origins in Lebanon. He also persuaded me that North Carolina home cooking should not be confined to barbecue or meat-and-threes when he took me to Neomonde.

In 1977, the four brothers in the Saleh family from Lebanon opened Neomonde as a small baking company. Over time the bakery grew and added a deli, which transformed into a full-fledged restaurant in 2000. The menu is classic Mediterranean, but it is genuine home cooking, so popular in Raleigh that it draws people from downtown and the suburbs to its off-the-beaten-track location near the State Fairgrounds.

FROM I-40 *If headed east*: Take Exit 289 (Wade Ave.). Follow Wade Ave. for 3 miles. Turn right onto I-440/US 1 South. Go 0.6 mile and take Exit 3. At the end of the ramp, turn left on Hillsborough St. Go 0.3 mile and turn right onto Beryl Rd. After crossing the railroad tracks, make an immediate left, and Neomonde is just ahead.

If headed west: Take Exit 293 onto I-440/US 1 North. Go 2.5 miles and take Exit 3. At the end of the ramp, turn right on Hillsborough St. Go 0.3 mile and turn right onto Beryl Rd. After crossing the railroad tracks, make an immediate left, and Neomonde is just ahead.

AFTER EATING The J. C. Raulston Arboretum, a nationally acclaimed garden with one of the largest and most diverse collections of plants adapted for landscape use in the Southeast, is a few blocks away at 4415 Beryl Rd.

....

Pam's Farmhouse Restaurant

5111 Western Boulevard, Raleigh, NC 27606 · (919) 859-9990
Monday–Friday 6:00 A.M.–2:00 P.M.;
Saturday 6:00 A.M.–12:00 P.M.; closed Sunday
MAY NOT ACCEPT CREDIT CARDS

The late Nancy Olson, the world-famous and beloved former owner and bookseller at Quail Ridge Books in Raleigh, told me about Pam's. "It's one of the best country cooking places, ever," she said. "It's got the best red-eye gravy, and there are always interesting people there." When we finally met there for lunch one day, I found out what she was talking about. The southern-style vegetables (collards, okra, and corn) that were offered with my fried chicken were perfectly cooked. I loved the banana pudding and wished that I had had a little more room.

"Pam Medlin has been in the business since she started busing tables at a restaurant that our family owned in Henderson," says Pam's mother, Peggy Robinson. That family tradition continues at Pam's. Her brother, Clay Wade, is a cook, and her sister, Tammy Edgerton, is a waitress. Some of the regular customers, who eat breakfast and lunch there every day, are like family, too.

FROM I-40 *If headed east*: Take Exit 289 (Wade Ave.). Follow Wade Ave. for 3 miles. Turn right onto I-440/US 1 South. Go 3 miles and take Exit 2B. See below for directions from Exit 2B.

If headed west: Take Exit 293 onto I-440/US 1 North. Go 2 miles and take Exit 2B. See below for directions from Exit 2B.

FROM EXIT 2B OFF I-440 At the end of the ramp, turn left on Western Blvd. Go 0.5 mile. Pam's will be on the left, but the divide prevents a left turn. Go 0.2 mile farther, make a U-turn at the traffic light at Heather Dr. to reverse course, and come back to Pam's.

. . . .

State Farmers Market Restaurant

1240 Farmers Market Drive, Raleigh, NC 27603 · (919) 755-1550
Monday–Saturday 6:00 A.M.–3:00 P.M.;
Sunday 8:00 A.M.–3:00 P.M.
realbiscuits.com

Although Gypsy Gilliam and her son, Tony, have added some modern dishes to the menu, the State Farmers Market Restaurant is still known for the incredible fresh vegetables, courtesy the state Farmers Market, the go-to spot for the region's best produce. But there's more to it. These folks also know how to cook it right: squash, greens, collards, beans, corn. And don't forget the biscuits or cornbread, iced tea, and friendly service.

The restaurant also has a museum-quality collection of old-time farm equipment. Civil War memorabilia and North Carolina historical objects line its walls. So even if the food were not so good, this place would be worth a stop. Everybody comes here to eat and meet—businesspeople doing deals, farmers taking a break from selling their crops at the market, working people, and lots of family groups having mini-reunion meals.

If I had one place in the state to take visitors from another country, just to show them what North Carolina was all about, I would bring them right here for the food, of course, but more than that, for the rich diversity and goodness of the North Carolina people who show up to eat here.

FROM I-40 Take Exit 297 (Lake Wheeler Rd./Dorothea Dix/Farmers Market exit). Head north for 0.25 mile, following the signs to the Farmers Market. The restaurant is the building with the big dome.

AFTER EATING Take a few minutes to walk around the market area. Even if you can resist the extra-fresh vegetables and other crops, you will enjoy the displays and shops. It is a mini–state fair. And if you miss the 3:00 P.M. closing time for the State Farmers Market Restaurant, try the Market Grill or the North Carolina Seafood Restaurant at the Farmers Market just a few steps away for a late lunch or supper.

· ·

Big Ed's City Market

220 Wolfe Street, Raleigh, NC 27601 · (919) 836-9909
Monday–Friday 7:00 A.M.–2:00 P.M.;
Saturday 7:00 A.M.–12:00 P.M.; Sunday 8:00 A.M.–1:00 P.M.
bigedscitymarket.com

This is where it all got started for me. In 1994, I wrote a column about my favorite country cooking restaurants. One of those was Big Ed's. Here is some of what I wrote back then:

> Big Ed's in downtown Raleigh. It ought not to work. A big country restaurant in the center of the city that is decorated with farm implements from 50 and 100 years ago. Waitresses in country dresses and Big Ed himself dressed up in old-time overalls and checked shirt. But it does work, even when it is overrun by big-time lawyers, politicians and other power people. When they come to Big Ed's they have to put aside their fancy facades and be like home folks again. Ed's waitresses overwhelm you with a rough-and-ready niceness that makes every customer feel real good—but not too important.

And years later, not much has changed.

Big Ed Watkins founded the restaurant in1958 and moved it to Raleigh's City Market in 1989. Writing in the *Huffington Post*, John Mariani captured the spirit of the place perfectly: "The tables are covered with gingham oilcloth and Big Ed himself is usually decked out in a gingham shirt and blue overalls. Yet nothing about the place seems, to use a Yankee word, kitschy. The friendliness of the greeting and the helpfulness of the waitresses (who will tell you that you ordered way too much) add vitality to a very mixed crowd of people, high and low, for whom eating here is the thousandth or first time."

My favorite dish? I shouldn't admit it, but I love better than anything one of Big Ed's biscuits, drenched with butter molasses. Here's to Big Ed's lasting another 25 years.

FROM I-40 Take Exit 299 for Hammond Rd. Turn left onto Hammond Rd., then continue on to S. Person St. Turn left onto E. Davie St., then right onto Blake St., then left onto Wolfe St. Big Ed's will be on your left.

AFTER EATING Visit the nearby shops and stroll in Moore Square, a part of the historic city plan. Great museums and the state capitol are within walking distance. If you are a barbecue lover, don't forget to check out the iconic Clyde Cooper's Barbecue, at 327 S. Wilmington St., and a more recent addition to barbecue experts' favorite list, The Pit, at 328 W. Davie St.

· ·

Stephenson's Bar-B-Q

11964 NC 50 North, Willow Spring, NC 27592 · (919) 894-4530
Monday–Saturday 10:00 A.M.–8:00 P.M. (9:00 P.M. in summer);
closed Sunday

This is a favorite eating place for popular mystery writer Margaret Maron, who lives nearby and is a distant cousin of the late Paul Stephenson, who started the restaurant. Paul's son, Andy, who took over a few years before Paul's death, now manages it. Even if you don't see Margaret Maron when you visit, you will surely see some of the models for the characters in her books among the diverse people who frequent the restaurant. When you're eating your chicken and barbecue and slaw, don't forget to leave room for the banana pudding.

I still remember my first visit to Stephenson's with Paul's brother Shelby, later made North Carolina's poet laureate. Paul was still alive, and Shelby's wife, Lynda, was in good health. Eating with Shelby and Lynda that night made me determined to find more of these perfect local places to eat and visit.

I couldn't get enough of the slaw—green cabbage, chopped fine, sweet-and-sour flavoring that gave just the right touch to go with the barbecued pork and chicken, Brunswick stew, fried chicken, and hushpuppies. All these were on our table along with big chunks of potatoes covered with a tomato sauce. We were eating and talking like crazy. And when my tea glass got empty, a smiling waitress had it filled before I could think to ask her. When I asked her for some more ice, she grinned and winked and pointed to the bucket that was already on the table.

All of a sudden I remembered some of my friends who travel I-40 to Wilmington, often going back and forth to the beach every weekend in the summertime. I remembered how they sometimes complained that, except for the fast food outlets at the intersections, there is no place on I-40 between Raleigh and Wilmington to stop for a good meal. Oh, if they could only be with us now, I thought. Stephenson's Bar-B-Q is only a mile and a half detour from the interstate. But sadly, only the "insiders" know where it is and how to find it.

Shelby told me about how his brother Paul gave up farming back in 1958, developed his own special cooking techniques and sauce, and opened this place for business. That Wednesday evening, Paul was at choir practice. "Paul loves to sing," Shelby said, admiringly. "And he will be singing somewhere every Sunday and lots of evenings too." These days you can't help but think Paul is up there, enjoying singing in some heavenly choir.

FROM I-40 Take Exit 319. Head west on NC 210 about 0.5 mile. At the intersection with NC 50, turn right and go 1 mile.

AFTER EATING Stephenson's is probably the only barbecue restaurant in the country that has a commercial nursery next door. Shelby Stephenson says Paul started "messing around" with plants not long after opening the restaurant and pretty soon was selling plants. The business grew and grew. Today the nursery business is strictly wholesale, but that won't keep you from checking it out after your meal.

Other eateries in the vicinity are described in the I-95 chapter, including Broad Street Deli and Market, Sherry's Bakery, The Diner, and McCall's Bar-B-Que & Seafood.

. . . .

The Redneck BBQ Lab

12101B NC 210, Benson, NC 27504 · (919) 938-8334
Open every day 11:00 A.M.–7:00 P.M.
TheRedneckBBQLab.com

New restaurants don't have a long life expectancy—a vast majority close before they're even a year old—and because of that, we don't normally consider them for inclusion in *Roadside Eateries*. But when an award-winning barbecue pitmaster comes up with a new barbecue joint with the words *redneck* and *lab*, and barbecue aficionados rave about their experiences, there has to be an exception. It helps that The Redneck BBQ Lab is located close to I-40 and even closer to I-95.

In addition to offering good Eastern-style barbecue and locally sourced traditional fixings, owner Jerry Stephenson, who has competed on Food Network's *Chopped Grill Masters*, has branched out, offering expanded choices of ribs, burnt ends, and smoked chicken. The team is always trying new approaches.

The meats and sides are prepared fresh each day. They brag that they "hand strip collards and bake cornbread from scratch each morning." There is a downside because when the meats are gone, they are gone, so it's a good idea to call to check if you are coming late in the afternoon or evening.

Still not convinced to give these rednecks a shot? Well, just so you know, these "cue heads" have competed in well over a hundred Kansas City BBQ Society competitions and snagged 20 Grand Championships and 11 Reserve Grand Championships. Not bad if I do say so.

Owner Jerry Stephenson (left) and the next generation of The Redneck BBQ Lab pitmasters, Elle Stephenson

With all the experimenting going on, my choice is still their loaded barbecue sandwich, loaded with 'cue and slaw at a reasonable price.

FROM I-40 Take Exit 319 for NC 210 toward Smithfield/Angier. Then turn left onto NC 210 East, following signs for Smithfield. In less than 0.5 mile turn right, and The Redneck BBQ Lab will be on the right.

AFTER EATING Ask Jerry to show you his barbecuing equipment and discuss his latest projects. Also take a few minutes to admire the vintage photographs of local Johnston County families working in fields, harvesting tobacco, or standing in front of old farmhouses. Antique tobacco baskets and signs adorn the walls, and hand-painted murals are outside.

Meadow Village Restaurant

7400 NC 50, Benson, NC 27504 · (919) 894-5430
Sunday and Wednesday 11:00 A.M.–2:30 P.M.;
Thursday–Saturday 11:00 A.M.–2:30 P.M. and 4:00 P.M.–8:30 P.M.;
closed Monday–Tuesday
meadowrestaurant.biz

Betty Womble from Sanford told me that busloads of folks ride over from Sanford to see the famous Christmas lights in Meadow and then stay to eat at Meadow Village. She raves about the seafood and the homemade desserts. "The chocolate pie is to die for; it's delicious. And there is a really nice salad bar."

Julia Raynor and her husband opened Meadow Village in 1982. Until her death in 2018, Julia watched over the operation even as she dealt with serious injuries stemming from a car accident in 2010. Although paralyzed from the waist down, she moved about the restaurant in a motorized wheelchair, bringing optimism and cheer to her customers. Today, Julia's son, Timmy, is proud of Meadow's low prices: under $10 for the lunch buffet and about $12 for the huge spreads in the evening and on Sunday at noontime.

Becky Lupton, who has worked at Meadow for 20 years, 5 years as manager, cheerfully greets guests at the door and collects advance payments for the bountiful buffet that awaits them.

"Don't miss putting Meadow in your book" is advice I got from countless friends for whom Meadow is a special treat on the way to the beach. Don't you miss it, either.

FROM I-40 Take Exit 334 and follow NC 96 toward Meadow for 0.7 mile. Turn left onto NC 50 and go about 100 yards.

AFTER EATING During the Christmas season, the lights in this tiny town attract visitors from all over Eastern North Carolina. The Bentonville Battlefield is about 15-20 minutes away, well worth a visit if you have never seen it.

*Meadow Village
Restaurant near
Benson*

. . . .

The Country Squire
Restaurant, Inn, & Winery

*748 NC 24 Business, Warsaw, NC 28398 · (919) 894-5430
Tuesday–Friday 12:00 P.M.–7:00 P.M.;
Saturday 12:00 P.M.–9:00 P.M.
countrysquireinn.com*

Maybe the Country Squire is a little too upscale to fit in the home-cooking category. But so what if it is a little fancy; it is still a gathering place for folks from all over Duplin County. My friend Tom Kenan says he makes a point to stop by for a meal whenever he visits Liberty Hall, the old Kenan family homeplace, now restored and open to visitors. Owner Iris Lennon, a native of Scotland, has given her restaurant, inn, and surroundings a festive European touch.

FROM I-40 Take Exit 364 and follow NC 24 Business (College St.) for about 3 miles, passing through Warsaw. Turn right onto NC 24-50 Business. Go 4 miles. Country Squire will be on the left.

AFTER EATING Visit the gift shop or ask Iris to give you a tour of her winemaking operation, and consider buying a bottle to remember your visit.

Billy's Pork & Beef Center

5716 S. NC 41, Wallace, NC 28466 · (910) 285-6047
Monday–Saturday 7:00 A.M.–7:00 P.M.; closed Sunday

Whole country hams hang in the window of Billy's Pork & Beef Center. For many years, visitors could watch Billy himself and his brother Kenneth making delicious sausages. When Billy died in 2017, three local couples joined forces to buy the business. Thanks to their efforts, visitors to the store and restaurant in the charming small town of Wallace can also examine a wide selection of products, including rubs, breading, sauces, and marinades. If that's not enough reason to stop by, you can stock up on high-quality meats, conveniently packaged and ready to go.

When you finish shopping, you can sit down to a meal of real pit barbecue and fixings—you can even watch the butcher cut a steak for you straight from a slab of Black Angus beef.

FROM I-40 Take Exit 384 for NC 11 and then turn right onto NC 11 S South. After about 2 miles turn left and then left again, and Billy's will be on the left.

AFTER EATING Take a quick trip downtown to visit the Wallace Commercial Historic District, a national historic district that primarily includes commercial buildings with examples of Queen Anne and Moderne-style architecture. Notable buildings include the former Wallace Post Office (ca. 1940–41), the old Farmers Bank & Trust Company (ca. 1922), White House Cafe, Wallace Depot and Freight Warehouse, Oscar Rivenbark Wholesale Building (ca. 1945), Johnson Cotton Company Building and adjacent Warehouse (ca. 1945), Blanchard Pontiac dealership (ca. 1945), and the former Robert Carr Gulf Station (ca. 1936).

Paul's Place Famous Hotdogs

11725 US 117, Rocky Point, NC 28457 · (910) 675-2345
Open every day 6:00 A.M.–9:00 P.M. (closes at 10:00 P.M. on Friday
and Saturday)

Paul's Place is not exactly a home-style restaurant, but the hot dogs are legendary. My friend Ben Barker (father of the famous former chef at Durham's Magnolia Grill) says it is a "must" stop. "These dogs are different. Go all the way with onions and slaw and his special sauce—not chili!"

Stewart McLeod, who edited the newspaper in Clayton, told me, "You can't leave out Paul's Dogs. . . . It's the best hot dog I've ever eaten. Once, while in college at UNCW, I ate five for lunch. Today, if I am in the area, I stop even if it's not lunchtime."

According to McLeod, the unique red relish at Paul's is "a hold-over from the World War II era when beef was rationed. Since your standard chili was not then an option, Paul's came up with its famous relish recipe."

Today, Paul's Place is "where the local men hang out to swap stories at lunchtime," a Castle Hayne resident told me. David Wilson Paul, the third-generation owner of Paul's, agreed: "I'll talk your ear off." His grandfather started Paul's in 1928. "Back then, they were open 24 hours a day. When my granddad died back in 1939, they had to nail the doors shut to close the place so they could go to the funeral. Before that, they never had any need for locks. It was always open."

Paul's still stays open most of the time. But it closes for a few hours at night. And Paul's has made one other concession to modern pressures: it now serves chili. "We didn't want to, but so many people asked for it, we just went ahead and added it."

David Jonathan Paul, the fourth generation of his family, took my order recently. He says nice things about all the state's college football and basketball teams, but if you mention NC State, his alma mater, he breaks into a wide smile. Paul's also serves a full breakfast

Paul's Place Famous Hot Dogs in Rocky Point

and has other items on its menu. But most people still stop just to get one of those famous hot dogs.

FROM I-40 *If headed east*: Take Exit 408. Turn left on NC 210. Go 0.3 mile to US 117. Turn left and go 3.5 miles. Paul's is on the right.

If headed west: Take Exit 414. Head west on Holly Shelter Rd. toward Castle Hayne. Go about 1 mile into Castle Hayne. At the intersection of Holly Shelter Rd. and NC 117, turn right (north) onto NC 117. Follow NC 117 going north for about 3 miles. Paul's is on the left.

AFTER EATING On weekends, a busy flea and farmers market sets up next door. It is a great place to meet local people.

Casey's Buffet

5559 Oleander Drive, Wilmington, NC 28403 · (910) 798-2913
Wednesday–Saturday 11:00 A.M.–9:00 P.M.;
Sunday 11:00 A.M.–8:00 P.M.; closed Monday–Tuesday
caseysbuffet.com

I first heard about Casey's from my friend Bob Woodruff, who stopped me one day at the grocery and said, "Hey, I've got the place for you. While we were at the beach last weekend, we were driving down Oleander in Wilmington and I saw the Casey's sign with the pig on it. That is usually a good omen."

He told me there was an all-you-can-eat buffet and that the restaurant was full of all kinds of people, mostly working folks. He said that the tab was $11.99 ($10.99 for seniors) with a buffet full of fried chicken, baked chicken, barbecue, whiting fish, and chitterlings. Every day, he exclaimed, they had pigs' feet. I told Bob it sounded like soul food, and he said it was. He liked the okra even though it wasn't fried. He did say there was one problem: "I got full before I was ready to stop eating!" Still, Bob found room to get a sample of two kinds of fruit cobbler before he left. It sounded too good to be true, but I found that Bob Woodruff had only scratched the surface of the good things to eat at Casey's.

I did a little research and found that Casey's is a nationally known soul food restaurant. One fan raved that it is "the real deal" and "a soul food-lover's dream come true. . . . They have pretty much everything: fried chicken, chitterlings, fatback, chops, okra . . . you name it. Unlike many buffets, everything is fresh, hot, and scratch-made."

Larry Casey and his wife, Gena, opened the restaurant in 2005. Previously, Larry had spent about 10 years at the Wilmington branch of Taste of Country before it closed.

Casey's has a slogan: "Miss ya Mama's cookin' . . . Come home to Casey's."

My wife, Harriet, and I loved everything on the buffet line, just as Bob Woodruff said. We could not believe how crisp and delicious the fried catfish tasted. Larry explained that he has a special source from a farm near Greenville.

"When UNC-TV's Bob Garner visited us," Larry told me, smiling, "he liked the catfish, too. And he mentioned our source in Ayden. All of a sudden, they couldn't supply us anymore because they had sold out to people who heard about it from Bob. But we've gotten that straightened out and they are taking care of us again." Larry told me that the best-selling vegetable is "okra, pan fried, unbreaded, and lightly seasoned, which I fashion after my grandmother Kitty Casey."

In 2019, *Reader's Digest* readers selected Casey's as North Carolina's favorite all-you-can-eat buffet. The magazine advised, "Make sure you come hungry so you can gorge yourself on the all-you-can-eat ribs, chitlins, chicken gizzards, catfish, collard greens, and hushpuppies. And if you're feeling really adventurous, you might even go for the pigs' feet, which are popular with the locals."

Something else was very special when my family visited. Even though Casey's was crowded with folks coming from church on that Sunday, people on the staff, including Larry and Gena, were extra friendly and helpful to every customer.

FROM I-40 Where it turns into N. College Rd. (US 117), follow N. College Rd. for 4 miles to Oleander Dr. Turn left and go 2 miles. Casey's is on the left.

AFTER EATING Now that you are in Wilmington, there is no limit to the "must visit" places to see. For instance, Airlie Gardens, with its 67 acres of historical gardens, is only about 2.5 miles away via Oleander Dr. and Airlie Rd. The nearby campus of UNC-Wilmington is lovely and worth a drive through. Even closer, in fact right across the street at 5570 Oleander Dr., you can take a few minutes to watch the hitting practice at Bats and Brews batting cages.

INTERSTATES 73 & 74

"Why don't you find us some home-cooking places near our new interstates I-73 and I-74?" Folks began to ask me this question a few years ago when the future I-73 and I-74 signs began to appear on some of our highways.

At first I resisted. It is tough enough to cover the locally owned, family-operated restaurants that are near enough to the "real" interstates to give an alternative to the fast food franchises that surround the intersections.

Then I looked at the proposed routes and saw that there would be some good gathering places to eat near the proposed routes—places like The Snappy Lunch in Mount Airy near I-74, made famous by Andy Griffith.

So let's give it a try. And if you are willing to go a little way off the interstate, you will find there is good eating at some nice friendly places along the way.

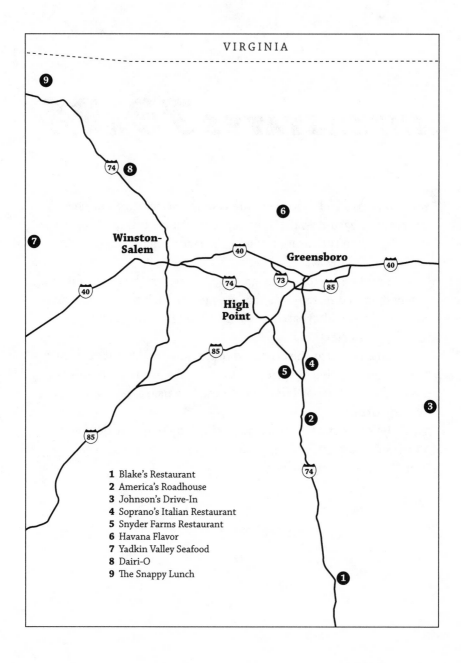

VIRGINIA

Winston-Salem

Greensboro

High Point

1 Blake's Restaurant
2 America's Roadhouse
3 Johnson's Drive-In
4 Soprano's Italian Restaurant
5 Snyder Farms Restaurant
6 Havana Flavor
7 Yadkin Valley Seafood
8 Dairi-O
9 The Snappy Lunch

Blake's Restaurant

127 Hillview Street, Candor, NC 27229 · (910) 974-7503
Monday–Friday 6:00 A.M.–8:00 P.M.;
Saturday–Sunday 7:00 A.M.–2:00 P.M.

In 1947, after Colon Blake came back from army service in France during World War II, he opened Blake's Restaurant. At first he bought an old truck stop, fixed it up, and opened up shop. Then, in about 1955, he built a new structure on old US 220 near Candor and Biscoe. The restaurant became a community gathering place and one of the best places to stop on that north-south route that runs right through the middle of North Carolina.

About 1985, when US 220 Bypass was built around Candor, Blake saw the handwriting on the wall. So he had his building moved 2 miles to its current location, where the bypass (now the new interstate) intersects with NC 211. I remember when I visited him a few years ago, Blake encouraged me to order the chicken pot pie, saying I ought not pass it up, but I selected another one of the specials. My fried chicken, butter beans, corn, and mashed potatoes were mighty good, and after I finished my special plate, Blake told me to try the coconut cream pie. When I said I was full, he said, "No, you have to try it. I'm going to pay for your dessert." That was a hard offer to resist. Made on the premises, it is as good a dessert as I can ever remember having.

When Blake became seriously ill in 2007 and died soon afterward, his staff and family rallied to show that, thanks to his mentoring, they would be able to keep his restaurant going strong, even if he were no longer there every minute to check on things.

FROM I-73/74 Take the NC 211/Candor exit. Head west on NC 211 toward Candor for a few hundred feet, then turn right into the Blake's Restaurant parking lot.

AFTER EATING In summer, visit one of the many fine peach orchards and stands near Candor. About 10 minutes south of Blake's is Johnson's Peaches at 1348 Tabernacle Church Rd., Candor. It is open most of the year, even when peaches are not available. Ken Chappell Peaches & Apples, Kalawi Farms, and other fine orchards are 5 or 10 minutes away on NC 211 going east toward Eagle Springs and are open seasonally from mid-June.

· ·

America's Roadhouse

818 E. Dixie Drive, Asheboro, NC 27203 · (336) 633-1234
Tuesday–Thursday 11:00 A.M.–9:00 P.M.;
Friday–Saturday 11:00 A.M.–10:00 P.M.; closed Sunday–Monday
americasroadhouse.com

My college classmate Bob Auman of Raleigh told me that he happened to find America's Roadhouse "by luck and by chance" while traveling through Asheboro and that he thoroughly enjoyed the oysters and the Hawaiian chicken salad.

On a recent visit Bob ordered the fried oysters. "One of the co-owners/co-managers said that fresh seafood from Louisiana is trucked in regularly. The oysters were super, and the serving was more than ample."

When I stopped by on a late Friday morning, it was almost full, mostly with seniors. But, said co-owner Joe Robertson, a different mix was going to keep them busy all weekend long. Joe and his partner, Andy Archibald, opened their business in 2002, after working together for other restaurants. "We thought we could do a better job on our own."

"What is your secret?" I asked. "Fresh seafood," he said. "We pile it high."

They also offer a "zoo menu" in honor of the nearby North Carolina Zoo, serving up ostrich, buffalo, alligator, and frog legs.

FROM I-73/74 Take the Asheboro/US 64 exit. Head east on US 64 toward Siler City and Raleigh. Go about 2 miles. America's Roadhouse is on the right.

Johnson's Drive-In

1520 E. Eleventh Street, Siler City, NC 27344
Note: no telephone and no drive-in service
Tuesday–Saturday 10:00 A.M.–2:00 P.M.; closed Sunday–Monday
MAY NOT ACCEPT CREDIT CARDS

Johnson's Drive-In is a long way from I-73/74 and, in fact, a bit far from any interstate. But it's worth the trip. For years, every time I saw him, Randy Gardner told me, "You mean you live so close, and you've never been to Johnson's? Their cheeseburger is the best in the world."

Then there were other legends about Johnson's that I wanted to check out. "Get there early. When he runs out, he closes. And it can be well before 2:00 P.M."

People explained that Johnson's owner estimates the amount of ground beef he needs for each day, grinds it fresh each morning, and when he runs out, that's it. There are no more cheeseburgers that day.

Other people told me that it was not the ground beef. He would shut down each day when he ran out of buns.

Former North Carolina House of Representatives speaker Joe Hackney backed up what everybody else said about Johnson's, adding, "You know, the owner, Claxton Johnson, is my cousin. And another cousin, Wade Hackney, eats there every day, same time each day, like clockwork. Get there early because Claxton really does run out—every now and then. Even if he doesn't run out, it gets mighty crowded at lunchtime, and you might not be able to find a seat."

"So," I asked Joe, "what is the secret of this special cheeseburger?"

"Well, one of these secrets is the big thick block of 'cheese' Claxton pushes down on top of the burger," Joe said. "And you know what it really is? It's Velveeta."

Having heard so much about Johnson's, I was ready when longtime friend Jamie May invited me to eat lunch with him there. When we arrived about 11:30, it was already crowded. But we found

Johnson's Drive-In in Siler City

seats at the counter. From there we watched Claxton presiding over the grill, making each burger individually on order.

"They taste different, you know, depending on what you put on the bun. A lettuce and tomato cheeseburger is an entirely different thing from one with chili and onions," Claxton told us. But the quick hint of a smile told me he thought his burgers were the best, whatever else he put on them.

"So what is the real secret to your cheeseburgers?" I asked.

"Mainly, it's the beef—midwestern, grain fed—ground fresh every day and put on the grill only when I get the order. And, everything that's not used on one day, meat, slaw, chili, or anything else, gets tossed out. I am not going to ruin that good beef with day-old slaw."

FROM I-73/74 Take the Asheboro/US 64 exit. Head east on US 64 toward Siler City and Raleigh. Go about 23 miles. Johnson's is on the south side of US 64 (Eleventh St.) where it intersects with E. Raleigh St.

AFTER EATING Consider experiencing the rich Latino culture in Siler City with a visit to Tienda Loma Bonita, a store and café at 214 Martin Luther King Jr. Blvd., not far from Johnson's, for a selection of imported food products. The Loma Bonita name comes from a town in Mexico in the Oaxaca area, the hometown of the owners who now live in Siler City. If you are still hungry, try an authentic Mexican dish at the café in the back of the store.

....

Soprano's Italian Restaurant

638 W. Academy Street, Randleman, NC 27317 · (336) 498-4138
Open every day 10:30 A.M.–10:00 P.M. (11:00 P.M. on Friday and
Saturday)

The man responsible for Soprano's and its reputation for solidly good Italian dishes is not Italian at all. Ossama Hashish hails from Alexandria, Egypt, but he has been in North Carolina for some time. He managed a restaurant in Asheboro for about 5 years before opening Soprano's in 2000. You don't have to sing for your supper, but you might sing Soprano's praises after a meal. The Italian food is great, and lots of customers order the lunchtime meat-and-two-vegetables special. Randleman is the original home of the famous auto-racing Petty family, and they still live close by, regularly ordering takeout from Soprano's.

FROM I-73 Take Exit 82 (Academy St./Randleman). Head east on W. Academy St. for about 0.5 mile, passing through a roundabout. Soprano's is on the left at the far end of a strip shopping center.

AFTER EATING The Petty Museum at 309 Branson Mill Rd., Randleman (Level Cross), is about 10 minutes away via I-73 headed north. Four generations of the Petty NASCAR racing family, Lee, Richard, Maurice, Kyle, and Adam, are featured.

Snyder Farms Restaurant

2880 Beckerdite Road, Sophia, NC 27350
(336) 498-3571 or, for catering, (336) 498-4872
Thursday–Saturday 5:00 P.M.–9:00 P.M.;
Sunday 11:30 A.M.–2:00 P.M.; closed Monday–Wednesday

This NASCAR-themed restaurant is a veritable temple to Richard Petty. When Petty's mother visited a few years ago, she exclaimed to her son, "Richard, they have more of your junk in here than you do at home!"

But it's the food that keeps locals coming back for supper on Thursday, Friday, and Saturday and lunch on Sunday. What food! Fried chicken, country ham, country-style steak, fried fish, hush-puppies, corn, slaw, and fried green squash. And homemade yeast rolls, biscuits, and banana pudding.

Betty Snyder, along with her late husband, Wayne Snyder, began serving the Randleman area in 1984, offering homemade fried chicken, fried squash, banana pudding, and other southern favorites. Their children, David and Annette, are helping continue the tradition.

Hal Powell, a frequent visitor, says, "Snyder's is probably the best buffet in the state! I surely think so!"

FROM I-74 (ALSO US 311 BYPASS) Take Exit 84 and turn right onto US 311. Go 0.5 mile and turn left onto Beckerdite Rd. Follow Beckerdite Rd. for 2 miles. Snyder Farms Restaurant will be on the right.

AFTER EATING Hang around the restaurant to be sure you have seen all the important Richard Petty memorabilia.

Other area eateries described in the I-40 chapter include
The Diner, Real Q, Sweet Potatoes, Plaza Restaurant, Prissy
Polly's BBQ, and Stamey's Barbecue. You'll find Pioneer Family
Restaurant and Steakhouse, Mary B's Southern Kitchen, and
Kepley's Bar-B-Q in the I-85 chapter.

Havana Flavor

4432 US Highway 220, Summerfield, NC 27410
(813) 263-0978
Tuesday–Friday 11:00 A.M.–5:30 P.M.;
closed Sunday–Monday

This is the first food truck we've included in *Roadside Eateries*, so you know it has to be good. If you're driving on I-73 north of Greensboro, do yourself a favor and go track down Havana Flavor, usually located at the Exxon on US 220. Owner and chef José Dominguez has brought real Cuban food to the Triad area—from Cuban sandwiches to shredded pork with sweet plantains—and I couldn't be happier. A real customer favorite is the Cuban Love Sandwich, a hot-pressed sandwich with ham, Swiss cheese, pickles, and guava jelly. It's not just Cuban food but José's love of cooking and his family that is so appealing. "My beginnings in Cuban cooking are from childhood," José told me. "In my country, Cuba, I was a nurse for a long time, although my inclination was always to cook. I learned from my grandmother, who turns 103 soon, and my mother, who I lost in 2022. I believe that a good cook, like a good carpenter, is not only someone who studies, but who has the inclination towards that art, as many painters have been great in history because of their painting, not because of what they studied." Wise words, José.

Now, usually we include restaurants in this guide with a long history of serving their community. Havana Flavor hasn't been around all that long, but I'd argue that it's in it for the long haul, which is just as good. José opened Havana Flavor just before the COVID-19 pandemic, and it's a family-run affair. José brings years of experience and a love for his community and family with every dish he makes. Make sure to check Havana Flavor's Facebook page for its current location and hours before your visit, as they do sometimes set up shop in other areas. The food will be worth the detective work, I promise you.

Havana Flavor food truck

FROM I-73 Take Exit 119 for US 220 South, then keep right to continue on Battleground Ave., about 2 miles. You'll need to make a U-turn at Summerfield Rd., then go 0.25 mile. Havana Flavor is a blue food truck located in the Exxon parking lot.

Another eatery in the area, Central Cafe,
is described in the I-77 chapter.

· ·

Yadkin Valley Seafood

154 Beroth Drive, Yadkinville, NC 27055
(336) 679-8191
Tuesday–Thursday 4:00 p.m.–9:00 p.m.;
Friday–Saturday 4:00 p.m.–9:30 p.m.;
Sunday 11:00 a.m.–9:00 p.m.; closed Monday

Yadkin Valley Seafood began its history in 1985 when Gus Janus, who grew up and learned his cooking skills in the Greek community in Winston-Salem, came to Yadkinville. He built a small building just off US 421 and did such good business serving seafood to locals and travelers that in 1997 he built a larger building clearly visible on the north side of the highway. Billy, son of Gus and his wife, Vivian, recently finished community college and was on the scene when I visited. It was clear his parents have prepared him to take charge should they ever decide to retire. I asked Billy what his customers' favorite dish is. "Everything," he asserted. He quickly added, "It's probably popcorn shrimp." I would add my vote for that dish, but other customers also recommend the fried oysters, hushpuppies, and flounder.

FROM I-77 Take Exit 73A to merge onto US 421 South toward Yadkinville/Winston-Salem. In 6 miles, take Exit 259 for Reavis Rd. Turn left onto Bethel Church Rd./Reavis Rd., then take a right onto Billy Reynolds Rd. In about a mile, turn right onto Beamer Rd. and continue onto Beroth Dr. Yadkin Valley Seafood will be on your left.

AFTER EATING Don't leave Yadkinville without visiting the downtown/courthouse area and the Yadkin Cultural Arts Center.

Another eatery in the area, Central Cafe,
is described in the I-77 chapter.

Dairi-O

365 E. Dalton Road, King, NC 27021 · (336) 983-5560
Sunday–Thursday 10:00 A.M.–10:00 P.M.;
Friday–Saturday 10:00 A.M.–11:00 P.M.
dairios.com

North Carolina public historian Fred Kiger grew up in the tiny Triad town of King, though he now lives in Chapel Hill. He remembers well the little drive-in that was Dairi-O. The original little drive-in opened in 1947. Though it's long gone now, a restaurant of the same name still stands in King. Kiger says, "New place, but same fantastic hot dog. When I go home, it is a must to make a pilgrimage to the Dairi-O. Get a couple dogs and take them home for my Mom and I to eat."

Looking back he remembers, "I was at the Dairi-O at least one time or two every week of my childhood. I had my first root beer there. The hot dogs have never been reproduced. Wonderful. The butter-toasted bun. The sweet-tasting slaw. Their homemade ice cream was the best—the black cherry was my favorite. I first remember going with my parents and in my dad's pride and joy— his '56 black and white Chevy Bel Air. It was only three or four miles from my house on Tobaccoville Road."

David Harrison, who also grew up in King, agrees that the place has a near-legendary status. His favorite from this reborn restaurant? The "unmatched strawberry milkshake," which comes loaded with strawberries and is made to order. "It takes me back to my childhood time after time," he says.

Another native of King, UNC-TV's Caroline Francis, remembers walking up the railroad tracks from her home to get a chocolate sundae at Dairi-O. She says that her mother, who still lives nearby, still loves the hot dogs.

But you don't have to have grown up in King to stop at Dairi-O. Anyone pulling off the interstate will be treated like a neighbor and delighted by the milkshakes and hot dogs.

FROM I-73 Take Exit 123 toward King and follow S. Main St. for about 2 miles into King. Turn right on E. Dalton Rd. Go 0.2 mile. Dairi-O will be on the left.

The Snappy Lunch

125 N. Main Street, Mount Airy, NC 27030 · (336) 786-4931
Tuesday, Wednesday, Friday 5:45 A.M.–1:45 P.M.
Thursday and Saturday 5:45 A.M.–1:15 P.M.
thesnappylunch.com

When I travel in other countries, I try to connect the people I meet to North Carolina by describing something they already know and then explaining the connection. I try things like tobacco and cigarettes, the Wright Brothers' first flight, Michael Jordan, Billy Graham, Bank of America, the Research Triangle Park, and so on. Lately, I have been thinking about mentioning former Davidson College basketball player Stephen Curry. Sometimes, but not often, one of these connective links works, but there is one that almost always does: Andy Griffith and Mayberry. "So you come from where Andy lived," they say. And I then have a new friend.

Maybe, then, a trip to Mayberry or Mount Airy, where Andy really grew up, should be on every North Carolinian's bucket list. A trip there would not be complete without a visit to The Snappy Lunch, where Mount Airy residents—like the real Andy and many others—have eaten since it opened in 1923. "Make it snappy," some customers said when they ordered a sandwich. Hence the name, The Snappy Lunch.

Longtime owner Charles Dowell created Snappy Lunch's classic, a pork chop sandwich described as "a boneless, tenderized loin chop dipped in sweet-milk batter and fried until golden crisp."

Although Dowell died in 2012 at age 84, his legacy still is felt. His widow, Mary, and daughter, Jamie, own and operate Snappy Lunch with help from Jamie's husband, Seth Dowell-Young, who is in charge of the grill, where Charlie used to hold court. The family is determined to keep Charlie's legacy alive. Mary's great-nephew, Brady Horton, took my order for the famous pork chop sandwich, all the way. He brought it to me wrapped in wax paper, almost dripping with juicy slaw, tomato, and sauce, with pork so large it was poking outside the bun.

The fare is simple and good, mostly sandwiches at lunch. Breakfast is served until 10:30 A.M. Raymond Keith Massey was eating breakfast while I ate my sandwich. He told me he came "five times a week." When I asked why so often, he said, "It's cheap, two eggs and a big piece of pork, just $2.14."

Massey then told me that he really came for the fellowship. He admires Mary for taking care of others. "If you ain't got no money, you can eat for free. Mary just says to them, 'Somebody else has already paid for you.'"

Remember: Do not leave without sampling that pork chop sandwich. It's worth the trip.

Lynn York, author and leader of the book publisher Blair, grew up in nearby Pilot Mountain. In her debut novel, *The Piano Teacher*, she wrote about a small-town restaurant called the Squeezebox. Its real name was the Luncheonette, but it was crowded at lunch, hence the nickname. Because she writes about "a grill full of sizzling pork chops and fried baloney," could Snappy Lunch have made its way into her novel, renamed as the Squeezebox?

FROM I-74 Take Exit 11 onto Rockford St. toward Mount Airy. Go 3 miles to Graves St. (on the left). Turn left onto Graves St. Follow Graves St. (which becomes Dixie St.) for 0.2 mile to Franklin St. Turn right and follow Franklin St. for 0.1 mile. Turn right on N. Main St. (a one-way street) and go 0.1 mile. Snappy Lunch will be on the right.

AFTER EATING Walk up and down Main St. Visit the City Barber Shop and ask who cut Andy's hair. At 301 N. Main is the Mount Airy Museum of Regional History, and a few blocks away at 218 Rockford St. is the Andy Griffith Museum. Both museums charge a reasonable admission fee.

INTERSTATE **77**

"Isn't it about time that you came home, D. G.?" I was glad to get this question. It is always nice when someone from your hometown says they wish you would move back.

"Oh, no," a friend said, "I meant that you should write about some of the good home-cooking places to eat around here—next time you do one of your interstate eating books."

Maybe she was right. I traveled all across North Carolina on the interstates trying to find good home-style places to eat near the intersections. Not the fancy, new places but the old restaurants, cafés, and local gathering places. I tried to find places where the locals eat and where visitors are made to feel at home.

But I neglected I-77, the road that runs right through the town where I grew up, the city where I practiced law for 20 years, and the place my wife and I raised our children. These are places where my North Mecklenburg High School football teammates Tommy and Donnie Ohler and their dad, J. W., first introduced me to their great barbecue, now famous thanks to the annual Mallard Creek Barbecue. Finally, as a result of two close but unsuccessful campaigns for the U.S. Congress, I learned more about the fellowship and friendship building at local eateries than I did about winning elections.

So my friend was right. I should not neglect the places where my love of fellowship and food had arisen.

Following my friend's suggestion, I gathered a few of my old favorite places along I-77 and some new ones to share with you.

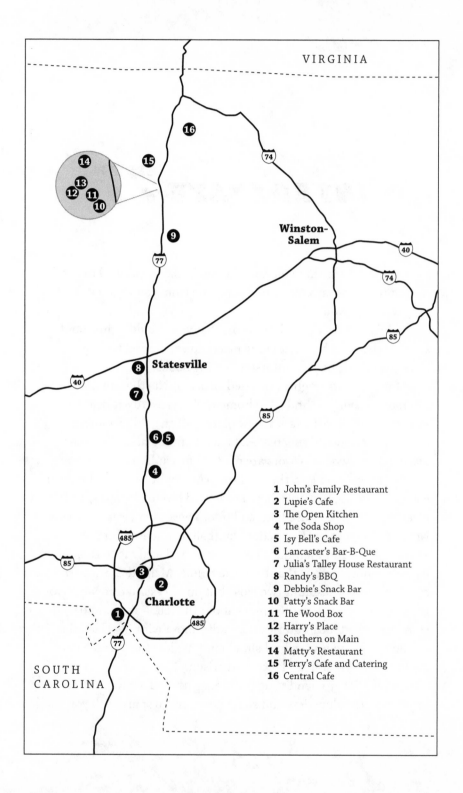

VIRGINIA

Winston-Salem

Statesville

Charlotte

SOUTH CAROLINA

1 John's Family Restaurant
2 Lupie's Cafe
3 The Open Kitchen
4 The Soda Shop
5 Isy Bell's Cafe
6 Lancaster's Bar-B-Que
7 Julia's Talley House Restaurant
8 Randy's BBQ
9 Debbie's Snack Bar
10 Patty's Snack Bar
11 The Wood Box
12 Harry's Place
13 Southern on Main
14 Matty's Restaurant
15 Terry's Cafe and Catering
16 Central Cafe

Maybe this chapter will help you find a pleasant place to stop and eat. If it does, then we can both be glad that I did go home again.

I-77 takes us from the crowded urban areas where Charlotte spills over into South Carolina all the way to the sparsely populated mountain border with Virginia. Along the way, I will guide you to a couple of genuine home-cooking restaurants in the Charlotte area, take you to a sandwich shop in my hometown, give you an option to eat family-style in a historic house, show you where local old-time music and food come together, and give you a chance to eat in a small county-seat community.

· ·

John's Family Restaurant

2002 Westinghouse Boulevard, Charlotte, NC 28273 · (704) 588-6613
Monday–Saturday 11:00 A.M.–9:00 P.M.; closed Sunday

If you visit John's Family Restaurant on Wednesday nights, you will join folks who are stopping by after church choir practice to get a plate of southern home-style vegetables. The owner, John Tsoulos, makes a promise on the menu: "No Canned Vegetables." Or at lunchtime you can stand in line with crowds of folks who work in the industries and offices that line Westinghouse Boulevard and the nearby areas of southern Mecklenburg County.

John specializes in local, southern-style food. But it didn't come naturally. He grew up in Greece, left school and went to work at age 10, got a job on a cruise ship, jumped ship in New York in 1970, and made his way to North Carolina.

"It's all right to talk about it now. I have been legal for a long time. And everybody knows I love America," John told me when I stopped by to sample his food.

John's customers love him, too. They admire the way he is always working. "You would never know he is the owner from the way he cleans off tables, checks the orders, and backs up his crew wherever he is needed."

John's Family Restaurant has been open at this location for about 20 years. Earlier he occupied the building across the street where another restaurant is now located. The "new" home is bright, clean, very comfortable, and big enough to seat up to 250 people—almost enough to take care of the lunchtime crowd.

I learned about John from former state senator Fountain Odom, who lived nearby for many years and says that John is one of America's great success stories. And I learned from John that he loves to talk to his customers about his love of hard work and fresh southern-style vegetables and, most of all, his love for America.

FROM I-77 Take Exit 1 (Westinghouse Blvd.). From the intersection, head west on Westinghouse Blvd. (If you are headed south, it will be a right turn off the long exit ramp; if you are going north, turn left.) Go about 1.5 miles. John's Family Restaurant is on the right, at the intersection with Pioneer Dr.

Another eatery in the vicinity, United House of Prayer for All People, is described in the I-85 chapter.

· ·

Lupie's Cafe

2718 Monroe Road, Charlotte, NC 28205 · (704) 374-1232
Monday–Friday 11:00 A.M.–10:00 P.M.;
Saturday 12:00 P.M.–10:00 P.M.

Guadalupe (Lupie) Durand learned how to cook simple foods from Lillie Mae White, the cook at the old Thompson Orphanage in Charlotte. Lupie went to live at Thompson Orphanage when she was 13. "She pretty much cooked everything from scratch," Lupie remembers of Lillie Mae. Since Lupie's opened in 1987, its simple, homemade, inexpensive dishes have drawn a diverse and loyal set of fans. "I started making chicken and dumplings because it was cheap. But people like things plain and simple."

Lupie's may be best known for its chilies. It has three different ones: Texas, Cincinnati, and vegetarian. But the honest food and surroundings, Lupie's welcoming spirit, and the diverse and friendly folks who fill up the restaurant have always made mealtime a happy time for me.

Lupie's daughter, Larkin, has come to help her mom and recently introduced a chicken casserole to Lupie's offerings.

For me, the best thing about Lupie's is the variety of it customers: bank presidents, former governors, flight attendants, and ordinary folks like you and me.

FROM I-77 *If headed north*: Take Exit 9 (US 74 East/I-277 North/ John Belk Fwy.). Follow I-277 for 2 miles. Take Exit 2B onto US 74 East (Independence Blvd.) Follow Independence Blvd. for 2 miles. Turn right onto Briar Creek Rd. Go 0.5 mile. Turn right onto Monroe Rd. Go 0.5 mile. Lupie's is on the left.

If headed south: Take Exit 11 (for I-277 South/Brookshire Fwy. East/ NC 16 South). Merge left onto I-277 South. Go 1.8 miles. Bear left to take Exit 2B (US 74 East/East Independence Blvd.). Follow Independence Blvd. for 2 miles. Turn right onto Briar Creek Rd. Go 0.5 mile. Turn right onto Monroe Rd. Go 0.5 mile. Lupie's is on the left.

AFTER EATING Just a few blocks away at 2700 E. Independence Blvd. is the Bojangles Coliseum (originally Charlotte Coliseum). When it opened in 1955, it was the largest unsupported steel dome in the world. Still looking like a giant spaceship, it is worth a drive-by.

The Open Kitchen

1318 W. Morehead Street, Charlotte, NC 28208 · (704) 375-7449
Monday–Tuesday 11:00 A.M.–9:00 P.M.;
Wednesday–Thursday 11:00 A.M.–9:30 P.M.;
Friday 11:00 A.M.–10:00 P.M.; Saturday 4:00 P.M.–10:00 P.M.;
Sunday 4:00 P.M.–9:00 P.M.
worldfamousopenkitchen.com

Even from a distance of miles and time, whenever I remember my visits to The Open Kitchen as a teenager, I think about the red-checked tablecloths, the brick walls, the old political buttons, post-cards, celebrity photos, and college pennants on display—each one put up individually over a long period of time. And I remember how special The Open Kitchen was when I was in high school and college. The food was good, filling, and reasonably priced. And the folks who ran the place and those who worked for them were friendly.

It is still pretty much the same today, and it is therefore, for me, a welcome place to go back in time.

New Year's Eve in 1959 was one of the low points of my life. Our Davidson basketball team was struggling. We had been clobbered by Wake Forest and Tennessee. Our coach had lined up a "pushover" game for us against Erskine. Because the college was closed for the holidays, we played the game in a small gym in Mooresville. Under-dog Erskine trounced us. It was so bad that the coach even let me play at the end of the game.

Humiliated, we made our way to The Open Kitchen to try to "celebrate" the New Year. As soon as we arrived, we ran into "Big Bill" Ward, the WBTV sports anchor, and he told us we ought to cheer up, because "you all are going to be great—someday." That helped. What helped more was a group of telephone operators who had worked the evening shift and had come to The Open Kitchen for their New Year's Eve party. When they learned that we were basketball players, they treated us like heroes rather than losers. "We are Southern Belles," they laughed. And we laughed, too. And Davidson basketball has been on the upswing ever since. Awash in all these personal memories, I thought of something that is important to you: The Open Kitchen is just a few blocks off the interstate. And no hungry, lonely traveler should pass it by.

Stephanie Kokenes is the fourth generation of her family to work in the restaurant business in Charlotte. Her father, Alex, manages The Open Kitchen. Her grandfather Steve and his brother opened the restaurant in 1951. And her great-grandfather Constantine ("Gus") ran the Star Lunch in downtown Charlotte beginning in the early 1900s. Another of Gus's great-grandchildren, Stephanos Skiouris, is the son of Christina Skiouris, a co-owner.

All that tradition comes together at today's Open Kitchen, which got its name because Steve Kokenes wanted his customers to feel free to look inside the kitchen to see how the food was being prepared. That tradition still holds. Longtime employee Sue Brandon, who served our group cheerfully, is another tradition. When I asked why she'd stayed at Open Kitchen so many years, she told me, "It is just a good place to work—it's like home."

The food is home style too, Italian home style, even though the Kokeneses originally came from Greece. Sue Brandon told me that the lasagna is the most popular dish among the "regulars." But John Malatras, who has worked with the family for many years, says that their pizza is still a big favorite. "You know, they introduced pizza to Charlotte back in 1952. And people would come from all over just to try it out. It is still good!"

FROM I-77 *If headed north*: Take Exit 9 and then Exit 9C, following signs to US 74 West for 0.2 mile, and take Exit 1A to merge onto Freedom Dr. Go about 0.5 mile and turn right onto W. Morehead St. Open Kitchen is on the left. (Note that getting back on the interstate going north is really easy. Ask for directions at the Open Kitchen.)

If headed south: Take Exit 10A (Morehead St.). At the end of the ramp, turn right onto W. Morehead St. Follow W. Morehead St. for about 3 blocks. The Open Kitchen is on the right. Just before you get there, you will see a big, colorful sign that says "Alte! The Open Kitchen." The restaurant and its parking lot are just a few doors away. (To get back on the interstate going south, ask for directions at the Open Kitchen.)

The Soda Shop

104 S. Main Street, Davidson, NC 28036 · (704) 896-7743
Monday–Thursday 10:00 A.M.–8:00 P.M.;
Friday–Sunday 8:00 A.M.–8:00 P.M.
davidsonsodashop.com/menu.php

The Soda Shop's former owner, Deborah Caudle, explained the restaurant's special charm to me like this: "If you crave nostalgia or want to drift back to your college days or childhood, this is the place. The walls may not talk, but they tell a story of the history of the restaurant and customers."

In 2018 Caudle sold the Soda Shop to longtime employee Misty Utech, who promised to keep the old photos on the wall and preserve the other reminders of the old days. You might think I am suggesting The Soda Shop just to get you to stop in my hometown of Davidson. While it's true that I want to share that wonderful place with all my friends, The Soda Shop would be well worth a stop even if it weren't right in the middle of one of the nicest towns in the world.

You know you're in a college town when you walk in the door and see pennants and sports photos on the walls. For me the experience is extra special because The Soda Shop is almost exactly like the M&M Soda Shop that served Davidson students and townspeople while I was growing up. And when I order orangeade and an egg salad sandwich, it is a miracle. They are just as good as when Murray Fleming and Mary Potts made them for me more than a half-century ago. They cost a little more today, but they are still worth every penny.

The refreshing fruit drinks, the sandwiches, and the ice cream make The Soda Shop special, especially since Deborah expanded the offerings to include a wide variety of dishes. But what I like best is that you can stop at any booth and folks will treat you like a long-lost friend.

The Soda Shop in Davidson

The author of an article in *Garden & Gun* magazine called the M&M "a holy spot." I agree.

FROM I-77 Take Exit 30. From the intersection, head east on Griffith St. toward Davidson. Go about 1.5 miles, until you reach a dead-end at the Davidson College campus about a block after you cross the railroad tracks. Turn right on N. Main St. Go about 2 long blocks. The Soda Shop is on the right in the center of Davidson's small business district.

AFTER EATING Take a walk down the friendliest Main St. you will find anywhere. If you have an extra few minutes, take a short walk across the Davidson College campus. I bet you will start to understand why I am so glad that "I can go home again." But be careful—if you stay in Davidson much longer, you won't want to leave.

Isy Bell's Cafe

1043 N. Main Street, Mooresville, NC 28115 · (704) 663-6723
Monday–Saturday 6:00 A.M.–9:00 P.M.;
Sunday 8:00 A.M.–2:00 P.M.

The first thing I noticed about Isy Bell's Cafe was the sign on the outside. It said in big bold letters "HOME COOKING," and I knew I had come to the right place. Isy Bell's is near Mooresville's downtown, which is more than just a little way from the interstate intersections.

With all the development near the interstates, even some of the old Mooresville residents have forgotten about their local restaurant treasures. Thank goodness for Phil Alexander at the Iredell County Solid Waste Disposal Facility, who finally told me, "D. G., if you want real home cooking, then there's no question but that you have got to go all the way into town and try Isy Bell's. That is where they all go."

So off I went, winding myself away from I-77, around the northern edge of Mooresville, and then into the downtown area along North Main St. A little bit outside the main business center I found my "home cooking" sign.

I opted for the special plate with four vegetables and iced tea. I got mashed potatoes with great beef gravy, cabbage, corn, a combination of okra and tomatoes, and a biscuit and cornbread—perfect!

After I finished my great vegetables, I looked around the room and saw an old friend, the late Presley Brawley. Presley had campaigned for me when I was a political candidate many years ago. "D. G., I tried," he said, "but you came in here and told the dairy farmers that they needed to help clean up the streams that ran alongside their pastures. And you told all my hunting friends that they had to get involved in the gun safety movement. All that did not sell too well up here. We liked you, and we tried to help all we could. But you didn't make it easy."

I laughed, but I did have to ask Presley how he could just jump me with all of his complaints so many years after the campaign had ended—almost before he told me hello.

"Well," he said, "I'm now the senior member of the Iredell County bar, and I can say just about whatever I want, whenever I want—and I do." We had a good laugh about that.

Presley wasn't reticent about talking about the food at Isy Bell's Cafe either. "Take the selection of vegetables first," Presley said. "They have 20 different vegetables listed, and they will all be fresh. If you come in the morning you'll be surrounded by contractors. They get in here and meet and get their work lined up and make deals with each other. It is like a contractors' hall."

He then told me, in no uncertain terms, not to forget about the desserts. He was right about that. The peach cobbler had a wonderful bread-like crust that complemented the sweet, fresh peaches inside. Pressley told me that the strawberry cobbler is even better. But Isy Bell's owner, Mike Kabouris, had to give me the bad news: he had just run out of that dish. I guess it just gives me one more reason to go back to Isy Bell's—as if I needed another reason.

FROM I-77 Take Exit 36 (Mooresville/NC 150). From the intersection, head east on NC 150 toward Mooresville. Go through a very developed area for about 3.5 miles until you reach the intersection of NC 150 and NC 801 (W. Park Ave.). Turn right on W. Park Ave. and follow it for about 1 mile until it intersects with N. Main St. (also NC 152). Turn left and go about 0.5 mile, passing a Food Lion store just before you reach Isy Bell's Cafe, on the right.

AFTER EATING Make your way to 215 N. Main St. to see the Charles Mack Citizen Center, said to be "Mooresville's premier event venue." It honors the father of John Mack, former head of Morgan Stanley, who gave $4.5 million to expand the center. Charles Mack's father, also named John, came from Lebanon in 1903. He came to Mooresville by accident when a railroad agent in New York put him on the wrong train. He peddled clothing for a living, and one of the rooms in the Citizen Center is named the "Peddler Room" in his honor.

Lancaster's Bar-B-Que

515 Rinehardt Road, Mooresville, NC 28115 · (704) 663-5807
Sunday–Thursday 11:00 A.M.–9:00 P.M.;
Friday–Saturday 11:00 A.M.–10:00 P.M.
lancastersbbq.com

Lancaster's proudly serves Eastern-style barbecue right in the middle of Lexington-style barbecue territory. Owner Jim Lancaster got his start in the food business as a teenager in Louisburg, North Carolina, in 1964. For almost 40 years he has been cooking his style of barbecue. It is mighty fine, but the special reason to visit is a chance to celebrate Mooresville's close connections to the stock-car racing industry. The restaurant is decorated with racers' uniforms, flags, photos, and full-size racing cars. Lancaster's even has a full-size school bus on the floor, with tables inside for those who want to eat there. Lots of locals eat here, along with plenty of the famous race car drivers.

FROM I-77 Take Exit 36. Head east on NC 150. Go 2 miles, crossing US 21, to NC 152. Immediately turn left onto Rinehardt Rd. Lancaster's will be on the left.

AFTER EATING Don't leave Lancaster's without inspecting all the displays and decorations that celebrate the local connection to stock cars and their drivers.

Julia's Talley House Restaurant

305 N. Main Street, Troutman, NC 28166 · (704) 528-6962
Monday–Friday 11:00 A.M.–2:00 P.M. and 5:00 P.M.–8:30 P.M.;
Saturday 5:00 P.M.–8:30 P.M.; Sunday 11:00 A.M.–2:00 P.M.
juliastalleyhouse.com

"It is like Sunday dinner, but Grandma doesn't have to cook," Eric Wilkinson of Mooresville told me as he and his wife, Jennifer, waved goodbye to his parents, grandmothers, a great-great aunt, and another carload of relatives heading back to Lincolnton after a family meal at Julia's Talley House in Troutman.

"It is just a great place for us to come from different places and meet," Eric continued. "And my great-great aunt says the food is even better than it used to be." Julia's has been around since 1979, when Julia Shumate first opened her restaurant in the former home and office of a beloved family doctor. In fact, Dr. Talley had delivered Julia. So she honored his memory by putting Talley in her restaurant's name.

Approaching the entrance, I walked up to Dr. Talley's front porch. The rocking chairs were full of folks who had finished their meals and just wanted to visit a little longer. Just inside the house is a big portrait of Julia, who, until she died a few years ago, checked on things at the restaurant nearly every day.

Julia Shumate is gone, but her restaurant is still owned and operated by Shumate family members Kim, Joe, and Chris, who currently manage the day-to-day operations.

Inside, Julia's is still more like a house than a restaurant. And Eric Wilkinson was right. I got a family-style meal that was served just like an old-time Sunday dinner. They served me 10 different bowls of food, family-style, even though I was eating alone. If I had not been so hungry, I could have gone to the cafeteria line, paid a little less, and eaten more modestly. But I will choose family-style at Julia's every time. At suppertime and for the noontime meal on Sundays, Julia's fills up with families, both locals and people coming from miles around. At weekday lunchtime, things move a little fast, and Julia's provides a bargain meat-and-vegetable plate that includes iced tea. What to eat at Julia's? Fried chicken is its specialty, and it was great. But the country ham made the meal. The vegetables are better in the summer when more of them are fresh, but the plentiful selection will always give lots of good choices.

FROM I-77 *If headed north*: Take Exit 42 (US 21/Troutman). At the end of the ramp, turn left and head north toward Troutman on US 21 and NC 115. Go for about 3 miles to Troutman. Just beyond the small downtown of Troutman you will see Julia's Talley House on the left.

If headed south: Take Exit 45 (Troutman). Follow the signs to Troutman. Here is what you will do: At the end of the ramp, turn right onto Amity Hill Rd. Then after a few hundred yards, turn left onto Murdock Rd. Follow Murdock Rd. for about 2 miles until it dead-ends into US 21/NC 115. Turn left (south) on US 21/NC 115 toward Troutman. Just before you reach Troutman's downtown, you will see Julia's Talley House on the right.

Other eateries in the area, including Keaton's BBQ, are described in the I-40 chapter.

. . . .

Randy's BBQ

213 Salisbury Road, Statesville, NC 28677 · (704) 873-4444
Monday–Saturday 10:30 A.M.–8:00 P.M.; closed Sunday
CASH AND CHECKS ONLY
randysbbqnc.com

The bad news is that after 32 years, Carolina Bar-B-Q owners Gene and Linda Medlin closed their restaurant in 2017. I miss them, and not just because of their great Lexington-style shoulders cooked over wood coals. Gene's great sense of humor always made the restaurant a memorable stop. He told the story of Charles Kuralt's report that Gene's barbecue didn't have enough fat and gristle in it.

In response, Gene wrote a note he hung at the counter and told his customers that he would, upon request, add as much fat and gristle as anybody wanted.

Sad to lose the Medlins, but there is good news! There is still good barbecue to be had at the same location. Robin and Randy Pittman, owners of Randy's Bar B Que in Troutman, have opened a branch of Randy's at the Carolina Bar-B-Q site.

The Pittmans know the barbecue business well. Ironically, Randy got his start in this same building when it was owned by the legendary Gary Ritchie, the owner of Gary's in China Grove. Randy says that Gary is still a friend and an inspiration.

Visitors will notice that Robin and Randy have changed the inside of the building to give it a 1950s feel. But thank goodness, the barbecue is still good, even though Charles Kuralt might still ask for a little more fat and gristle.

FROM I-77 Take Exit 49B toward Statesville/Downtown and in less than 0.5 mile turn right onto Salisbury Rd. Randy's will be on the right.

AFTER EATING Take about a 3-block walk to the Statesville Civic Center at 300 S. Center St., where you can view renowned North Carolina artist and Statesville native Ben Long's fresco titled *Images at the Crossroads*. It features Hecate, a Greek goddess associated with crossroads, appropriate because I-77 and I-40 meet at Statesville. But Hecate is also associated with magic and witchcraft, which created an interesting controversy when the fresco was first displayed. Nearby, you can also stop to look at the old city hall, constructed around 1890. North Carolina architecture expert Catherine Bishir writes that architect Willoughby Edbrooke's building embodies "romanesque monumentality at its most handsome and restrained."

Debbie's Snack Bar

3008 Rocky Branch Road, Hamptonville, NC 27020 · (336) 468-8114
Open every day 6:00 A.M.–10:00 P.M.

We miss the combination of good food and good music that Myles and Pat Ireland served up at the Cool Shack in Union Grove. The music can't be replaced, but for a quick bite of country cooking, Debbie's might be better.

There are lots of things to like about this small, modest place that has been around since 1961. It is just off U.S. 421's Exit 264 and easy to find. The home-style cooking is bountiful, good, and reasonably priced. What I like best, though, is that it is a happy place. Its family atmosphere is almost overpowering as cheerful young servers rush in and out of the kitchen area. Debbie's doesn't pretend to be anything other than a small diner populated by locals, but I felt very welcome, and my smiling waitress made the food taste even better.

FROM I-77 Take Exit 73A to merge onto US 421 South toward Yadkinville/Winston-Salem. After a mile, take Exit 264 for Asbury Church Rd. Continue on to turn right onto NC 1126 East/Asbury Church Rd. Turn left onto Rocky Branch Rd. and then turn right, and Debbie's will be on the right.

AFTER EATING Swing by the nearby gas station for a fill-up. It has a reputation for low prices.

Patty's Snack Bar

124 N. Bridge Street, Jonesville, NC 28642 · (336) 526-1374
Monday–Thursday 11:00 A.M.–4:00 P.M.;
Friday 11:00 A.M.–8:00 P.M.; Saturday 11:00 A.M.–3:00 P.M.

How does a billiard business transform into a thriving little snack bar? I found out from Patty Cox Smith, the owner of Patty's Snack Bar.

Several years ago her friend Brian Haynes was operating a successful pool table repair shop and pool hall but noticed that some of his customers were leaving at noon to eat lunch somewhere else. Problem was, they didn't come back after they ate.

Something about this had to change. So to keep his customers from leaving, Brian persuaded Patty to organize a small, simple food operation right there in the hall. Pretty soon the food took off. Brian decided to move the repair and maintenance part of the business downstairs so Patty could use the entire main floor for the newly minted Snack Bar.

Now the pool hall is gone, too, and Patty's has a full menu that includes her famous hot dogs. You'll also find her Carolina Burger, made with fresh ground chuck brought in daily, served in a combo with mustard, onions, chili, and slaw.

On your way there enjoy a leisurely drive past the Brushy Mountains. Don't hurry! Just slow down and take in the view.

FROM I-77 Take Exit 82 for NC 67 toward Elkin/Jonesville/Boonville. Turn left onto NC 67 West. Drive for 1.5 miles, then turn left onto N. Bridge St. Patty's will be on your left.

AFTER EATING Get Patty to tell you about *That Little Big Paper*, the small local newspaper she produces in addition to running the Snack Bar. Be sure to pick up a copy and read about some of the goings-on about town. It's still free after all these years.

The Wood Box

401 N. Bridge Street, Jonesville, NC 28642 · (336) 526-4227
Monday and Thursday–Saturday 11:00 A.M.–8:00 P.M.;
Sunday 11:00 A.M.–2:30 P.M.; closed Tuesday and Wednesday

About four years ago, Alan and Cindy Hicks took over as owners of The Wood Box. The solid concrete building has a long history of serving up delicious barbecue, beginning in 1951. The piles of wood and smoky atmosphere outside let you know that the day's barbecue will taste of hickory.

Don't let the red awnings and cow statue fool you! This barbecue is serious business.

Alan has held many jobs, including in high tech, but he says he has been interested in smoked meats since he was a teenager. At his combination smoker and cooker, he turns out barbecued pork shoulders, ribs flavored with whiskey sauce, and what he claims are "better than Texas" briskets. Alan couldn't be prouder of the meat his smoker produces.

The Hickses believe their slogan, "Where fresh is best, taste everything," conveys their professional approach to serving customers the very best smoked meat products.

Alan admits that he charges just a touch more than some other barbecue places that don't use the wood smoke process, but the loyal customers that fill up the Wood Box certainly think it's worth it.

Or maybe it's the peach cobbler that keeps bringing them back. Either way, you can't go wrong.

FROM I-77 Take Exit 82 for NC 67 toward Elkin/Jonesville/Boonville. Turn left onto NC 67 West and drive 1.5 miles. The Wood Box will be on your left.

AFTER EATING You'll be well within walking distance of the Yadkin River, which separates Jonesville from Elkin and Yadkin County from Surry, so get a look at the river that was such an important feature in Daniel Boone's early life.

Harry's Place

135 Front Street, Elkin, NC 28621 · (336) 835-9693
Monday–Friday 11:00 A.M.–1:30 P.M.;
Wednesday, Friday, Saturday 4:30 P.M.–9:00 P.M.; closed Sunday

Around 60 years ago Harry and Nancy Smith opened what would become one of North Carolina's premier casual dining spots. Teresa Smith, Harry's daughter, is now the owner and continues the family tradition of serving tasty food at affordable prices. The classic railroad bridge near the eatery was inspiration for the restaurant's logo. I've been told Harry's is the best hole-in-the-wall you will ever find, and while it's hard to disagree, it's so much more than that for the many visitors who make their way there.

The menu may be small, but it doesn't disappoint. The ribeye is certainly a favorite, but people who live on the coast say they have yet to find crab legs as good as Harry's. Dishes come with a baked potato and salad, which most diners get topped with a house-made creamy Italian dressing.

If you can, try to get there early (especially on Pork Chop Tuesdays) because cozy is definitely the word here. There are only nine tables in the entire place, so don't be surprised if you end up sitting with a stranger. Remember, though, they won't be a stranger by the end of the meal.

FROM I-77 Take Exit 82 for NC 67 toward Elkin/Jonesville/Boonville. Turn left onto NC 67 West and drive 1.7 miles, then turn left onto Elm St. Turn right onto US 21 Business North, then turn right onto Commerce St. and continue onto Standard St. Turn right onto Fuller St., and Harry's Place will be on your left.

AFTER EATING Take a walk on a little section of the North Carolina Mountains-to-Sea Trail, which begins in the Blue Ridge Mountains, passes through Elkin, and continues toward the Outer Banks.

Southern on Main

102 E. Main Street, Elkin, NC 28621 · (336) 258-2144
Tuesday–Thursday 11:00 A.M.–9:00 P.M.;
Friday–Saturday 11:00 A.M.–10:00 P.M.;
Sunday 11:00 A.M.–2:30 P.M.
southernonmain.com

Marla Stern opened Southern on Main in downtown Elkin a few years ago. The small, neat restaurant might be more upscale than an ordinary eatery, but it is a welcome retreat for many downtown Elkin workers who take advantage of its high-quality vegetables and other traditional southern offerings, such as fried chicken, shrimp and grits, and fried green tomatoes. There is an extensive wine list and a favorite dessert specialty, the blackberry (or sometimes apple) "song," which is the Surry County word for cobbler.

Marla told the *Elkin Tribune*, "We're aiming for an experience that's not too casual but not too fine dining. Anybody can enjoy it. It can still be a date night place. I don't think we have enough of those here in Elkin. We get a lot of variety, which is good, but I was trying to fit a niche that wasn't being covered as much in town."

When I had a chance to talk to her, Marla explained to me that many travelers from I-77, and people from all over Jonesville and Elkin, drop by for a simple lunch. Visitors include race car drivers, members of the fire department from Elkin and Jonesville, farmers, and many retirees. At present, they are not able to serve breakfast, but Marla is looking at that possibility as a good opportunity.

FROM I-77 Take Exit 82 for NC 67 toward Elkin. Then continue to turn left onto NC 67 West. In less than 2 miles, turn left onto Elm St. and then right onto W. Main St./US 21 Business. In less than 0.5 mile, turn right onto E. Main St., and Southern on Main will be on your right.

AFTER EATING Explore the offerings at the nearby Elkin Antiques and Collectibles Mall at 131 S. Bridge St. This town landmark was built in the 1930s and is listed on the National Register of Historic Places. Home to more than 60 vendors, it includes a year-round Christmas shop and a record and comic book shop. Surely there is treasure to be found here for everyone.

. . . .

Matty's Restaurant

1111 N. Bridge Street, Elkin, NC 28621 · (336) 527-4644
Monday–Saturday 11:00 A.M.–8:00 P.M.; closed Sunday

Rev. Matt Ponce De Leon, known to the locals as Pastor Matty, who serves the Arlington First Baptist Church in Jonesville, owns Matty's Restaurant.

He and his manager, Eric Long, have been working together since they both cooked at another eatery almost 15 years ago. The restaurant seats about 90 and is still often crowded with locals and tourists who enjoy the Philly cheesesteaks, barbecue, and various seafood offerings. Don't forget to check the specials board for daily dishes.

The staff is so cordial and caring that you might think you are eating at Pastor Matt's church. Listen carefully and you can hear bits of religious music coming through the speakers.

The kids' menu has something for even the pickiest eater, and each choice includes a free drink and cookie. I've heard the popcorn shrimp is an especially popular choice for younger diners.

FROM I-77 Take Exit 82 for NC 67 toward Elkin/Jonesville/Boonville. Turn left onto NC 67 West and drive 1.7 miles, then turn left onto Elm St. Turn right onto US 21 Business North. In 1.8 miles, Matty's will be on your left.

Terry's Cafe & Catering

1000 US 21, State Road, NC 28676 · (336) 874-2791
Monday–Saturday 6:00 A.M.–2:00 P.M.;
Friday 6:00 A.M.–8:00 P.M.; closed Sunday

The easiest way to spot Terry's Cafe & Catering? Look for the
"Go Hog Wild" neon sign shining brightly on the front wall. I can't
think of a better slogan for this State Road eatery.

But don't take just my word for it. One of Terry's biggest fans
is Bill Freeman, the barber just a few doors down in the same shopping center. He has been eating at Terry's for about 8 years. "Every
day," Terry says, "he usually eats two meals there. He loves the
chicken pot pie on Mondays, the chicken Creole on Wednesday,
and the specials on every other day."

Another favorite is Terry's Burger, hand-pattied ground beef
with melted cheese, onions, mayo, and lettuce on buttery Texas
toast. The barbecue is a perfect balance of tart and sweet, and at
breakfast there is special gravy right out of a cast-iron skillet. But
for my money, the key to getting the most out of any stop at Terry's
is enjoying some of his prized homemade potato chips.

The cafe often draws clientele from the Hugh Chatham Memorial Hospital and the nearby State Road Animal Hospital (just the
staff, not the animals).

FROM I-77 Take Exit 83 for US 21 Bypass toward Roaring Gap/
Sparta. Continue on US 21 Bypass for 2.4 miles, then continue onto
US 21 North. In 2 miles, Terry's will be on your right.

Central Cafe

304 N. Main St., Dobson, NC 27017 · (336) 356-2100
Monday–Saturday 6:00 A.M.–9:00 P.M.; closed Sunday

Sadly, one of my favorite county-seat restaurants closed several years ago. The Lantern, with its home-cooked vegetables, fried chicken, meats, oysters, pulled pork sandwiches, and a changing array of reasonably priced meat-and-two-vegetables plates, was an institution.

Thankfully, another soon-to-be institution has opened in the same location. Noel and Julie Easter have moved their Central Cafe from its former location near the high school to the Lantern location. The Easters were well known for their work at other nearby restaurants, as well as their restaurant's classic American dishes.

Lantern customers will find good meat-and-vegetable-plate options much like the Lantern. But the hamburger plates and meat loaf plates are local favorites.

FROM I-77 Take Exit 93 toward Dobson and then turn right onto Zephyr Rd. After about 3 miles, continue onto W. Kapp St. In about 0.5 mile turn left onto N. Main St. Central Cafe will be on your right.

AFTER EATING Dobson is surrounded by some of North Carolina's finest wineries. But if time is limited, you can still enjoy a quick visit to the downtown and old courthouse.

INTERSTATE 85

I-85 just might be North Carolina's main street. It joins our state's major urban areas, and because its intersections are so crowded by development, the search for old-time home-cooking places can be frustrating. Still, there are many opportunities to sit down with local people along the way. You can sample barbecue not only in Lexington but also in Gastonia, Rowan County, High Point, Hillsborough, Durham, Butner, Henderson, and Norlina.

Since the first edition of *Roadside Eateries* was published, we lost a few of the most important barbecue joints in the state. Indeed, the closure of Nunnery-Freeman Barbecue, just off I-85 in Henderson, concluded an important chapter in North Carolina barbecue history. Owner Gary Freeman's father, the original owner, invented a barbecue cooker that many restaurants used to cook a good product without the backbreaking "cooking over wood coals" method. Thank goodness nearby Skipper Forsyth's Bar-B-Q is still cooking good barbecue, among many other good, down-home places.

If barbecue is not your thing, I will take you to a variety of other places to mingle with the locals and eat home-style cooking.

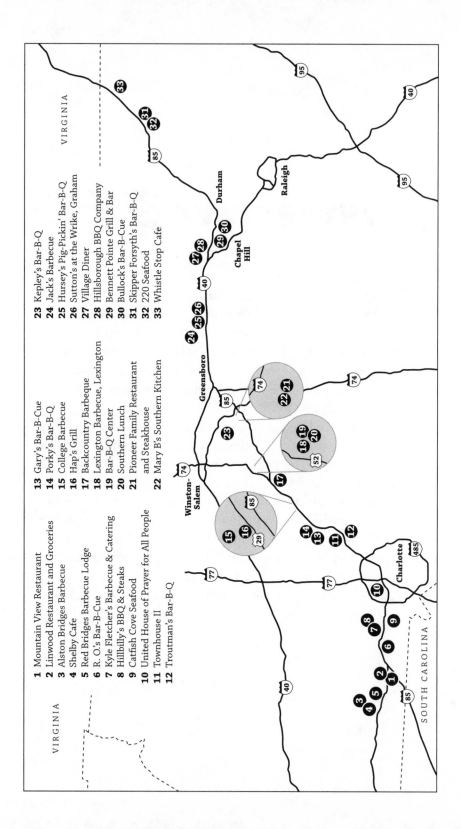

VIRGINIA

VIRGINIA

SOUTH CAROLINA

1 Mountain View Restaurant
2 Linwood Restaurant and Groceries
3 Alston Bridges Barbecue
4 Shelby Cafe
5 Red Bridges Barbecue Lodge
6 R. O.'s Bar-B-Cue
7 Kyle Fletcher's Barbecue & Catering
8 Hillbilly's BBQ & Steaks
9 Catfish Cove Seafood
10 United House of Prayer for All People
11 Townhouse II
12 Troutman's Bar-B-Q

13 Gary's Bar-B-Cue
14 Porky's Bar-B-Q
15 College Barbecue
16 Hap's Grill
17 Backcountry Barbeque
18 Lexington Barbecue, Lexington
19 Bar-B-Q Center
20 Southern Lunch
21 Pioneer Family Restaurant
   and Steakhouse
22 Mary B's Southern Kitchen

23 Kepley's Bar-B-Q
24 Jack's Barbecue
25 Hursey's Pig-Pickin' Bar-B-Q
26 Sutton's at the Wrike, Graham
27 Village Diner
28 Hillsborough BBQ Company
29 Bennett Pointe Grill & Bar
30 Bullock's Bar-B-Cue
31 Skipper Forsyth's Bar-B-Q
32 220 Seafood
33 Whistle Stop Cafe

Mountain View Restaurant

100 W. King Street, Kings Mountain, NC 28012 · (704) 734-1265
Tuesday–Friday 6:30 A.M.–9:00 P.M.;
Saturday 7:00 A.M.–9:00 P.M.;
Sunday 11:00 A.M.–3:00 P.M.; closed Monday

If you are traveling back and forth to South Carolina, Mountain View is a good place to say "hello" or "goodbye" to small-town North Carolina. In the winter, you can get a good view of Kings Mountain, where the patriots won an important battle in the American Revolution. Although Mountain View is a relatively new restaurant, the owner, Nick Mantis, former head cook at the Athens Restaurant in Charlotte, and his daughter, Georgia, the manager, have earned a loyal local clientele for their country cooking, lunch specials, and tasty Greek dishes. The law office of North Carolina Speaker of the House Tim Moore is nearby, and he is a regular for breakfast.

FROM I-85 *If headed north*: Take Exit 8 and follow NC 161 toward Kings Mountain for 1.5 miles. Turn left at E. King St. and go 0.5 mile. You will see the restaurant at the intersection of King St. and Piedmont Avenue.

If headed south: Take Exit 10B and follow US 74 West for 1.5 miles. Exit onto E. King St./US 74 Business West and follow E. King St. for 1.5 miles. You will see the restaurant at the intersection of King St. and Piedmont Ave.

AFTER EATING Assuming that you don't have time to visit the Kings Mountain Battlefield Park, walk a few blocks to the Kings Mountain Historical Museum at 100 E. Mountain St. It is open Tuesday–Friday until 4:00 P.M. Free admission.

Linwood Restaurant and Groceries

805 Cleveland Ave., Kings Mountain, NC 28086 · (704) 739-7308
Monday–Friday 7:00 A.M.–2:00 P.M.;
Saturday 7:00 A.M.–11:00 A.M.; Sunday 11:00 A.M.–2:00 P.M.
CASH ONLY

You might rightly go right past Linwood Restaurant and Groceries, just a few minutes' drive from the I-85 exit, without thinking it's a good place to eat. For one thing, the unassuming and faded sign says "groceries and produce," plus the building itself is what the young folks these days might call "rustic." But the food is worth stopping for, I assure you, especially if you want to get a good dose of local culture along with your meat loaf and butter beans.

Linwood is a true greasy spoon and serves up all kinds of tasty southern food that locals love. Warren Bingham, author of *George Washington's 1791 Southern Tour* and onetime resident of Kings Mountain, says that locals call Linwood Restaurant the Linwood Country Club. Now, it's not clear why they do, exactly, since there are no golf courses or swimming pools in sight, but maybe it's because longtime owner and chief cook Keith Falls has long been active in the community and treats everyone like they're part of an exclusive club. His catering business serves special events and civic clubs throughout the region.

Whether it's at the restaurant or at a catered event, people like Keith's food because it tastes good and is prepared with heart. If you stopped in after church, you'd see the community gathered at Linwood for Sunday supper. If that isn't a sign of a good place to eat, I don't know what is.

There are two more things you should know about Linwood Restaurant and Groceries. The first is that they're a cash-only business. The second is that, if you're searching for it online, it might come up as "Linwood Produce," but don't let that stop you from making your way through charming Kings Mountain to find that good, old-fashioned country cooking.

FROM I-85 Take Exit 8 for NC 161 toward Kings Mountain and then turn left onto James St. Turn left immediately and Linwood Restaurant and Groceries will be there.

· ·

Alston Bridges Barbecue

620 Grover Street, Shelby, NC 28150 · (704) 482-1998
Monday–Thursday 10:45 A.M.–8:00 P.M.;
Friday 10:45 A.M.–8:30 P.M.; closed Saturday–Sunday

Shelby tourist officials promote the rivalry between two cherished local barbecue joints, Alston Bridges Barbecue and Red Bridges Barbecue Lodge (described further below). "Award-winning BBQ and part of the unspoken BBQ war in Cleveland County," they say. "With two Bridges Barbecue restaurants you will have to decide which is your favorite."

Some refuse to decide. Ron Rash, famous author of the best-selling novel *Serena,* grew up nearby. When asked about his favorite place to eat, he says simply, "Bridges Barbecue in Shelby."

The two Bridges families are not blood kin, but they are bound together heritage-wise. Barbecue expert Jim Early says both Alston Bridges and Red Bridges learned their craft of cooking pork shoulders over hickory coals from the legendary Warner Stamey, the godfather of Lexington-style barbecue (which some people say should be called Shelby-style barbecue). Alston was Stamey's brother-in-law. As Warner Stamey's grandson Chip Stamey explained in John and Dale Reed's *Holy Smoke,* "All us barbecue guys are inbred."

Alston's grandson Reid Bridges and Red's granddaughter Natalie Ramsey agree that each has a loyal set of customers and there is plenty of business to keep both families busy.

So, which is better, Alston's or Red's? Locally, both have their loyal followers. Some are so loyal that they have never eaten at the "other Bridges." But consider visiting both and making your own decision. I've eaten at both places, and I am going back several more times before I make up my mind.

FROM I-85 Take Exit 10B and follow US 74 West about 15 miles to Shelby to the intersection of US 74 and NC 18 (S. LaFayette St.). Turn north toward Shelby and follow NC 18 (LaFayette St.) for 2 miles to the intersection with E. Grover St. Turn right to follow NC 18 and E. Grover St. Go 0.7 mile. Alston Bridges is on the right.

AFTER EATING Visit downtown Shelby. See the entry for Shelby Cafe.

....

Shelby Cafe

220 S. Lafayette Street, Shelby, NC 28150 · (704) 487-8461
Monday–Friday 7:00 A.M.–8:30 P.M.;
Saturday and Sunday 7:00 A.M.–3:00 P.M.

There are plenty of reasons to visit Shelby Cafe. Locals connect here, breakfast is available all day, and solid meat-and-vegetable plates are served at lunch and supper. But livermush, a combination of various parts of the pig flavored with spices, is my main reason for leading you here. Thanks to North Carolina food guru Bob Garner's book *Foods That Make You Say Mmm-mmm*, I learned the cooks at Shelby Cafe "will prepare your livermush pretty much to order, and they'll serve it inside a fluffy biscuit, next to fried eggs and grits, worked into a livermush and cheese omelet, or muddled into a breakfast casserole with eggs, cheese, mushroom soup, and sautéed onions."

Shelby businessman David Royster introduced me to Shelby Cafe owners George Rizkallah and Bryan Greene, who served me a plate of crispy, juicy livermush so good that I wake up at night wanting to taste it again.

Livermush is a popular local food in the western Piedmont and one of those things you have to eat to be a "real North Carolinian." The Shelby Cafe makes this initiation rite a pleasant one.

FROM I-85 Take Exit 10B and follow US 74 West about 15 miles to Shelby to the intersection of US 74 and NC 18 (S. LaFayette St.). Turn north toward Shelby and follow NC 18 (LaFayette St.) for 0.7 mile. Shelby Cafe is on the left facing W. Arey St.

AFTER EATING Visit the museum at the Earl Scruggs Center in the old courthouse building at 103 S. Lafayette St., which "combines the life story of legendary five-string banjo master and Cleveland County native, Earl Scruggs, with the unique and engaging story of the history and cultural traditions of the region in which Mr. Scruggs was born and raised."

· ·

Red Bridges Barbecue Lodge

2000 E. Dixon Boulevard, Shelby, NC 28150 · (704) 482-8567
Wednesday–Saturday 11:00 A.M.–8:00 P.M.;
Sunday 11:00 A.M.–4:00 P.M.; closed Monday–Tuesday

About 10 years ago, on my first visit to Red Bridges's one day a little after noon, I sat at a counter and ordered a barbecue sandwich and sweet tea. Both were delicious. While I was eating, an older lady, dressed as if she were going to church, came in alone. She smiled and greeted the wait staff, and soon one of them brought her a plate with two hot dogs. She held up her hand to protest, saying, "You all know my doctor told me not to order hot dogs anymore."

"But Mama B., you didn't order them," the server said. "We just brought them to you."

"Well, if I didn't order them," she said, as she took a bite of the hot dog, "it will be okay to eat them, wouldn't it?"

I figured out that Mama B. was Lyttle Bridges, the widow of Red Bridges, and that this little drama played out regularly at the noon hour.

Lyttle and Red opened their first barbecue restaurant in 1946. When Red died in 1966, Lyttle ran the business until she retired at 80 years old. Red and Lyttle's daughter, Debbie Bridges-Webb, runs the business with help from her children, Natalie Ramsey and Chase Webb.

Jim Early, author of *The Best Tar Heel Barbecue: Manteo to Murphy*, saved his highest praise for Red: "The woodsy, smoky, nutty-flavored pork is tender to a fault and, with sauce, is THE BEST. . . . The tangy brownish-red sauce is tart with sweetness. The sweet and sour makes your tongue and taste buds tango and your soul happy. I love this stuff."

In the spring of 2015, *Garden & Gun* conducted a best-barbecue-in-the-South voter poll, patterned on the NCAA basketball tournament's "Sweet Sixteen." Red Bridges triumphed, winning the top spot. "Although based in a North Carolina town of less than 30,000," the editors said, "the sixty-six-year-old barbecue joint, known for its chopped pork shoulder, hushpuppies, and vinegar-sauced red coleslaw, managed to rally its fan base and come out on top of all five rounds." One taste and it's easy to see why.

FROM I-85 Take Exit 10B and follow US 74 West about 15 miles to Shelby to Red Bridges Barbecue Lodge at 2000 E. Dixon Blvd. (US 74). The Lodge is on the left. You will pass it and make a U-turn to reach it.

AFTER EATING Visit downtown Shelby. See the entry for Shelby Cafe.

. . . .

R. O.'s Bar-B-Cue

1318 W. Gaston Avenue, Gastonia, NC 28052 · (704) 866-8143
Monday–Saturday 10:00 A.M.–10:00 P.M.; closed Sunday
rosbbq.com

Gastonia native Stephen Bryant told me about this restaurant, which has been a part of Gastonia for more than a half-century. Stephen told me how his parents had courted there when you could get two "slaw burgers" and a Coke for 32 cents. His parents went back recently, and as they pulled up beside the restaurant, a carhop came out to serve them just the way they did so many years ago, when Stephen was no more than just a gleam in his parents' eyes.

The special today, if you can believe it, is still the slaw burger, a sandwich filled with slaw. But what slaw! Juicy with just the right amount of mayonnaise, it surprises with added tomatoes and some secret spices that give it a wonderful flavor. But you ought to try the barbecue and slaw combination for a real treat.

Robert O. Black, the R. O. in the restaurant's name, opened up shop in 1946. His son, Lloyd, ran the place for many years with the help of Mark Hoffman, Lloyd's nephew and R. O.'s grandson. Mark has taken the lead now, but Lloyd drops by regularly. Either can tell you about Gastonia history.

Has R. O.'s changed much since 1946?

"Throughout the years, we have modified our style none," Lloyd says. "People grew up eating here and now their children eat here and work here."

If you miss the old-time experience of the drive-in restaurant, do like Stephen's parents: wait outside and let the carhops come to you.

FROM I-85 Take Exit 17 (Gastonia/US 321 South). Head south on US 321 (N. Chester St.) and go 1 mile to Airline Ave. Turn right and go 1 mile. (Airline becomes W. Gaston Ave.) You'll find R. O.'s on the right.

AFTER EATING Less than a mile away at 300 S. Firestone St., at the corner of W. Second Ave., is Loray Mill, the site of a 1929 labor strike. The historic textile mill has been preserved and converted to a mixed-use community.

Kyle Fletcher's Barbeque & Catering

4507 Wilkinson Boulevard, Gastonia, NC 28052 · (704) 824-1956
Tuesday–Saturday 11:00 A.M.–8:00 P.M.; closed Sunday–Monday
MAY NOT ACCEPT CREDIT CARDS

Kyle Fletcher says he got his start cooking when a friend needed barbecue for a wedding reception. Then he leased the building that formerly housed Bland's Barbecue and revamped it for his "charcoal and hickory" method of smoking. I've heard some people just drive by to enjoy the smells that come from his old-time cooking. Weighing in on the "Eastern vs. Lexington" controversy, Kyle says, "I don't put nuthin' on my meat—except hickory and charcoal smoke. That way they've got an option to put whatever sauce they want on my barbecue." Lots of local people agree with Kyle, and sometimes you'll find them lined up to enjoy the generous and reasonably priced wood-flavored servings. Kyle brags about his restaurant's recognition as the "Best of Gaston" by the *Gastonia Gazette*.

FROM I-85 Take Exit 22 toward Cramerton/Lowell. Turn left onto S. Main St. Go 0.3 mile and turn left onto Wilkinson Blvd. Go 0.4 mile. Kyle's is on the left. You will have to make a U-turn at Westover St. to reach it.

AFTER EATING Across the street at 4520 Wilkinson Blvd. is All Things Collectible. It is jammed full of baseball trading cards, comics, toys, and other collectible things.

Hillbilly's BBQ & Steaks

305 S. Main Street, Lowell, NC 28098 · (704) 824-8838
Monday–Thursday 11:00 A.M.–9:00 P.M.;
Friday–Saturday 11:00 A.M.–9:30 P.M.;
Sunday 11:00 A.M.–3:00 P.M.
hillbillysbbqsteaks.com

My friend Al Brand from Charlotte worked for many years at Pharr Yarns in nearby McAdenville. The textile plant is still thriving, a proud North Carolina tradition, and he told me that Hillbilly's was one of the favorite lunch spots for folks who worked at the mill.

You'll see what he means when you walk in and see the cheerful checkerboard country tablecloths and the tables filled with locals. The Boston butts are cooking over hickory wood coals inside, and the aroma is worth the price of the meal.

Owner Gerald Duncan explained to me that their barbecue is a combination of Lexington and Eastern North Carolina styles—with a tomato-based sauce that has a touch of vinegar. Maybe a "purist" would object, but not me—I found their combination mighty tasty. Duncan says, "Our menu and comfortable atmosphere create a truly enjoyable dining experience. We treat everyone like family."

FROM I-85 Take Exit 23 (Lowell/McAdenville). Hillbilly's is at the intersection. If you are coming from the north, you will almost drive into the parking lot as you drive up the exit ramp. If you come from the south, you will turn left at the end of the exit ramp onto McAdenville Rd. Then cross the overpass, and you will see Hillbilly's on the left.

AFTER EATING In December, downtown McAdenville is transformed, with hundreds of thousands of twinkling lights turning the town into a spectacular holiday display, drawing thousands of visitors every evening. Even at other times during the year, a visit to the restored McAdenville Historic District is worth a trip to see more than 100 contributing buildings and structures, including an upscale destination restaurant, a coffee and tea shop, an organic and natural foods grocer, an ice cream parlor, and a nostalgic hardware and mercantile store.

....

Catfish Cove Seafood

1401 Armstrong Ford Road, Belmont, NC 28012 · (704) 825-3332
Tuesday–Thursday 4:00 P.M.–9:00 P.M.;
Friday 4:00 P.M.–9:30 P.M.; Saturday 3:00 P.M.–9:30 P.M.;
Sunday (buffet) 11:00 A.M.–3:00 P.M.; closed Monday
MAY NOT ACCEPT CREDIT CARDS
catfishcove.net

Fish camp restaurants used to be a staple in Piedmont North Carolina, and people in Gaston and Mecklenburg Counties still talk about the joys of family meals at Lineberger's Fish Fry. Lineberger's is long gone, but Raymond Stowe, who cooked at Lineberger's for 30 years, picked up the mantle at Catfish Cove. Stowe knew how to get the oil at exactly the right temperature to seal the outside of the fish and hold the flavor inside. On the Friday night I visited, Stowe, his son, Kent, and Kent's wife, Summer, were busy getting seafood platters from the kitchen to the customers who had filled up the restaurant. But Raymond took time to smile with pride when he told me about how he took his savings from working at Lineberger's to build his own family business.

Sitting at the next table were Bobby Benton, Gray Brookshire, Ray Oehler, and their spouses. They live in the Mallard Creek section of Charlotte, and they told me, "We live a half-mile from a chain seafood restaurant, but we drive 30 miles every week to eat at Catfish Cove."

They were enjoying the catfish platter, which is what I am going for next time. I had the senior platter with scallops, fried onions, hushpuppies, and unlimited trips to the salad bar, all for much less than $10. But my new friends from Mallard Creek told me it was the catfish that they loved the most.

On Sunday, things change at Catfish Cove. At lunchtime, the fish camp stops serving seafood and becomes an all-you-can-eat country buffet.

Sadly, Raymond died in 2018, but Kent and Summer have picked up the mantle and are carrying on the family tradition.

FROM I-85 Take Exit 26 and follow Belmont–Mt. Holly Rd. toward Belmont. Go 0.5 mile and bear right onto Central Ave. After 0.8 mile turn right onto S. Main St. and continue onto Armstrong Ford Rd. for 2 miles. Catfish Cove is on the left after you cross the river.

AFTER EATING Sit on the porch and enjoy the waters of the South Fork Catawba River. Less than 5 miles away is the much-admired Daniel Stowe Botanical Garden at 6500 S. New Hope Rd. On your way back to I-85 (Exit 26) stop at the lovely campus of Belmont Abbey College, founded in 1876 by Benedictine monks and home to more than 1,700 students.

....

United House of Prayer for All People

2321 Beatties Ford Road, Charlotte, NC 28216 · (704) 394-3884
Monday–Friday 11:00 A.M.–7:00 P.M.;
Saturday 9:00 A.M.–3:00 P.M.; Sunday 10:00 A.M.–4:30 P.M.

The late Bishop C. M. "Daddy" Grace, founder of the national United House of Prayer for All People, would be proud of this mission service of his church. The modestly priced southern food is served cafeteria-style in friendly surroundings and happily satisfies most visitors. Some soul food fans say it delivers the very best fried chicken, meat loaf, cornbread, sweet potatoes, and cabbage around.

Sunday worship at the House of Prayer is enthusiastic, with a brass band accompanying singing and dancing. That enthusiasm carries over to mealtime.

FROM I-85 Take Exit 37 to Beatties Ford Rd. and turn right and go 0.5 mile. House of Prayer will be on the right.

AFTER EATING Ask for more information about the church and for a look at the main meeting hall. Also, Johnson C. Smith University Campus is 1.8 miles south at 100 Beatties Ford Rd.

Other area eateries described in the I-77 chapter include John's Family Restaurant, Lupie's Cafe, The Open Kitchen, and The Soda Shop.

· ·

Townhouse II

1870 S. Main Street, Kannapolis, NC 28081 · (704) 938-8220
Monday–Friday 5:00 A.M.–6:00 P.M.;
Saturday 5:00 A.M.–2:00 P.M.; closed Sunday

You will have to turn a few corners to get there, but if you're looking for a place where the Concord and Kannapolis crowd gathers for breakfast and lunch, or if you're looking for a place to get a good country meal for a reasonable price, it's worth winding your way to what the locals call "Janie's Townhouse II."

Be ready to eat. As one customer, Beth Snead, told me long ago, "You had better be careful when you make your order. If you ask for the 'large' plate and eat it all, you will be so full that you are just going to want to crawl under your desk when you get back to work." It is still true today.

UNC–Chapel Hill School of Medicine's Dr. Pete Chikes practiced in Concord for many years. When he goes back to visit, one of his first stops is Townhouse II. "You can go in and see everybody and interact with them, folks from all walks of life," he says. "And the food is unbeatable."

Many years ago, when I first stopped by, it was the middle of the afternoon. People were coming in, filling the place up. I wondered why they were there at that hour. The late Janie Hall, the owner, explained that they were eating an early supper. They have to eat early because Townhouse closes at 6:00 P.M. Why so early? Well, to open at 5:00 A.M., Janie said she had to get up at 1:00 A.M. and needed to get to bed early.

Everybody misses Janie, but her husband, Gene, her daughter, Carmen Steen, and Carmen's daughter, Casey, all help keep the restaurant going. In 2015, Casey had a baby, Kaylee Rebecca Price, who is already visiting regularly and could become the family's fourth-generation connection to Townhouse II.

FROM I-85 Take Exit 58 (Concord/Kannapolis). Take the Concord/ US 29 South ramp. Continue for 0.5 mile to US 29A (S. Main St.). Turn right and go 2 miles.

AFTER EATING When you pull up to Townhouse II, you will notice a sign beside the restaurant featuring a scantily clad woman. Don't look for any such entertainment inside. The sign simply advertises a lingerie shop in the adjoining shopping area. Why not make a quick visit and look for a present for a loved one?

. . . .

Troutman's Bar-B-Q

362 Church Street, North Concord, NC 28025 · (704) 786-5213
Monday–Thursday 6:30 P.M.–8:30 P.M.;
Friday 6:30 A.M.–9:00 P.M.; Saturday 6:00 A.M.–9:00 P.M.;
Sunday 7:00 A.M.–3:00 P.M.

The late Raiford Troutman, Concord auto dealer and entrepreneur, founded this institution more than 50 years ago. Until his death in 2018, even in his 90s he stopped by daily to check things out and touch base with his daughter, Karen Barbie, who runs Troutman's the way her dad did. Like her dad, Karen takes pride in cooking barbecue the old-fashioned way. "We only use hickory wood to smoke our pork shoulders," she told me. "Our pitmaster slow-cooks each shoulder for twelve hours. The smoke produced by the coals slowly seeps into the meat for a true, pit-cooked taste in every bite."

Raiford Troutman insisted on cleanliness. His son, Keith, said,

Troutman's Bar-B-Q on Church Street in Concord

"Heaven is gonna be a cleaner place when we all arrive with Dad there now picking up papers and trash."

Their regulars like their red slaw, a mix of red and white cabbage with pimentos, tomatoes, and a sweetened vinegar-based dressing.

Troutman's at breakfast time is a popular place for regulars to gather and talk. What explains the crowds at breakfast? Maybe it is just a tradition. Maybe it is the full breakfast plates that some people promise are just as good as Troutman's wonderful barbecue.

Troutman's historic location is on Church St. in downtown Concord. There is a second location at 18466 NC 109 in Denton, but when Hillary Clinton came to Concord to campaign in 2008, she, like many candidates before and since, made a stop at the Church St. location.

FROM I-85 Take Exit 58 toward Concord. Follow US 29/US 601 South (Cannon Blvd.) toward Concord. Go 1.3 miles. Bear right onto NC 73, which turns into Church St. Follow Church St. for 1.3 miles. Troutman's is on the left.

AFTER EATING Drive by the First Presbyterian Church, a few blocks away, at 70 Union St. Built in 1927, it was designed by Hobart Upjohn, who, according to North Carolina architecture expert Catherine Bishir, combined "red brick walls, simple forms, and handsome classical detailing" in his work. It was an appropriate place for Charles A. Cannon to worship. During the 1920s, Mr. Cannon merged nine separate companies to form Cannon Mills Company. He built the world's largest household textile manufacturer, each day producing hundreds of thousands of Cannon towels.

· ·

Gary's Bar-B-Cue

620 N. US 29, China Grove, NC 28023 · (704) 857-8314
Monday–Saturday 10:00 A.M.–9:30 P.M.; closed Sunday
MAY NOT ACCEPT CREDIT CARDS

Gary's Bar-B-Cue must be good, says Debbie Mullis of Concord, "because every time I'm there you'll usually find county patrolmen, National Guard personnel, and plenty of blue-collar workers alongside the coats and ties of businessmen."

She's right, and Gary's has been a stopping point on the road between Charlotte and Greensboro for a long time, even though finding it from the "new" I-85 can be a little bit confusing.

Gary's is really a museum of times gone by. He has a collection of old advertising signs that he displays on the walls. Incredibly, he always has an old-time, fully restored Chevrolet Corvette, Ford Thunderbird, Volkswagen bus, or other classic vehicle displayed on the floor of the restaurant.

Don't be misled by the sign on the side of Gary's building that says "Cokes 5¢." It is just a reminder of days gone by. But you do get free refills.

Gary's specializes in barbecue, more or less Lexington style, and the crowds of people who visit there every day, both locals and travelers who somehow find their way from the interstate, show that Gary's barbecue is worth the trip.

Gary's does a big take-out business. It advertises a "Funeral Meal" with one-third pound of barbecue for each person, together with slaw, baked beans, and chips, for $6.50 a person. Twenty-five cents extra to add potato salad.

Once, when I paid my bill to my waitress at Gary's cash register, I asked if there was a senior citizens' discount. "Oh," she said, looking horrified, "there is, but once I've rung it up, it's too late."

Then she looked me sweetly in the eye and said, "You know, we're not allowed to ask folks if they are seniors even when they look old enough. Some people take offense. And, you, oh no! I never would have guessed."

She knew that she had made my day. I went back to the counter, left an extra tip, and walked out the door, holding my gray head high, a little bit giddy, thinking about Corvettes and drive-ins and days long gone by.

When I was back at Gary's recently on a Monday evening, the house was packed with cheerful eaters. Of course, I remembered to ask for my discount, and I got it.

FROM I-85 *If headed north*: Take Exit 68 (China Grove/Rockland/NC 152). From the intersection, turn left onto NC 152 and head west for about 0.5 mile. Follow signs to US 29 Bypass/US 601 South, and turn right on Madison Rd. as it loops around to US 29 Bypass/US 601 South. Follow US 29 Bypass/US 601 South for about a 0.5 mile. Gary's is on the left.

If headed south: Take Exit 68 (China Grove/Rockland/US 29 Bypass South). From the intersection, follow US 29 Bypass South for about 1.5 miles. Gary's is on the left.

AFTER EATING Tiger World, a "fun and educational place to experience endangered species up close and personal," is about 10 minutes away at 4400 Cook Rd., Rockwell. Call (704) 279-6363 to schedule a visit or get information.

Porky's Bar-B-Q

1309 N. Main Street, China Grove, NC 28023 · (704) 857-0400
Tuesday–Saturday 5:30 A.M.–9:00 P.M.;
Sunday 7:00 A.M.–9:00 P.M.; closed Monday

Porky's is only a minute or two from Gary's. Its current owner, Rick Register, is continuing the tradition of former owner Mike Reid, who insisted on cooking with wood, appealing to those barbecue fans who claim that it is not real barbecue if it is not "pit cooked."

Porky's takes its day off on Monday rather than Sunday, giving it a big edge on Sundays, when most of the barbecue places along I-85 are closed up tight. It also serves a variety of food other than barbecue, appealing to people who like home cooking but don't want to eat barbecue at every stop.

Finally, there is a matter of the slaw. As Elizabeth Cook, former editor of the *Salisbury Post*, once told me, "It's the only barbecue place I know of around here that offers Carolina-style slaw—red, vinegary—and what I call Virginia slaw—sweet and mayonnaise-based—like I used to get back home in Fredericksburg."

You won't be able to find "Virginia slaw" at many other places around here. Though a few nearby Porky's have closed, the original is still going strong.

FROM I-85 *If headed north*: Take Exit 68 (China Grove/Rockland/ NC 152). From the intersection, turn left onto NC 152, head west for about 1 mile to the first stoplight (keep straight, being careful not to take any exits). At the stoplight, take a hard left turn onto Main St. Just after that turn you will see Porky's on the right.

If headed south: Take Exit 68 (China Grove/Rockland/US 29 Bypass South). From the intersection, follow US 29 Bypass South for about 1 mile, then take the exit marked NC 152/US 29 North. The exit ramp merges with Madison Rd. and then immediately intersects with NC 152/US 29 North. Turn right and follow this road for about

0.5 mile to a stoplight. At the stoplight, take a hard left turn onto Main St. Just after that turn you will see Porky's on the right.

AFTER EATING For a nontraditional tourist stop, visit Copart Salvage Auto Auctions at nearby 1081 Recovery Rd. You will find a virtual museum of the history of American automobiles in all kinds of conditions. It is about a mile away from Porky's via Main St.; turn right onto US 29 and then left on Madison.

· ·

College Barbecue

117 Statesville Boulevard, Salisbury, NC 28144 · (704) 633-9953
Monday–Friday 7:00 A.M.–8:00 P.M.;
Saturday–Sunday 7:00 A.M.–3:00 P.M.

College Barbecue is a popular gathering place, especially at breakfast and lunch. Lots of faithful fans in Salisbury appreciate the chopped pork shoulders that have been cooked over hickory coals for hours and hours. The day I stopped by, owner Jay Owen and son Jason were building a shed for their hickory wood. Jay explained that the wood storage room in the restaurant was being converted into a second barbecue cooker needed due to increased demand on special occasions. Then he took me inside to show me the shoulders slowly cooking to be ready the next day.

Jay's uncle, David Koontz, opened College Barbecue in the 1960s and sold it to Jay in 1998. Jay and Jason and the other folks at College work to make you feel like you're back in a small-town eatery of 50 years ago. Their hushpuppies, sweet tea, soups, and french fries complement the wood-smoked barbecue.

FROM I-85 Take Exit 76 and head west into Salisbury. Follow E. Innes St. (US 52) into Salisbury and as it turns into W. Innes St. for 2.5 miles to an intersection with Statesville Blvd. on the right and Mahaley Ave. on the left. Turn right onto Statesville Blvd. College Barbecue will be on the left.

College Barbecue in Salisbury

AFTER EATING Drive by the nearby W. G. (Bill) Hefner VA Medical Center, a 484-bed facility at 1601 Brenner Ave., where countless veterans, including my father, who died there in 1974, have been well treated and cared for. Catawba College, alma mater of former governor Pat McCrory, is just a few blocks away on Innes St.

. . . .

Hap's Grill

116 ½ N. Main St., Salisbury, NC 28144 · (704) 633-5872
Monday–Saturday 11:00 A.M.–4:00 P.M.; closed Sunday

Hap's Grill is a favorite of my friends from Salisbury, and I will admit I got some criticism for not including it in the first edition of *Roadside Eateries*. It is true that people line up on the sidewalk on N. Main St. at lunchtime. Salisbury native Wyndham Robertson has been a big promoter of Hap's, telling me that there was some drama surrounding the last Hap's hot dog at a family gathering. "When only one hot dog was left," she says, "there was quite a competition for it from various family members. My niece wryly observed that dividing up the family silver was simple by comparison."

But I resisted the call to add Hap's. It was hard to call Hap's a gathering place when there was no place to sit down, but I've since been shown that people gather there all the same, so I yielded, and Hap's is joining a few other popular stand-up hot dog icons in this new edition. And at Hap's during the warmer months, there is an outdoor table where customers can gather and visit.

Why is Hap's so popular? Great hot dogs and hamburgers, of course, and they are served with ice-cold Cheerwine, the soft drink invented in Salisbury.

Randy Gardner, my friend who's traveled all over the state as a salesman, is passionate about Hap's because the hot dogs are so good. He's argued that Hap's belongs on my list of the 20 North Carolina iconic eateries. He says, "I always go to Hap's whenever I'm on I-85 near Salisbury. Hamburgers, hot dogs, and soda pops only. No 'special sauce,' no pickles, no peppers, no lettuce, no tomatoes. And no french fries either. Just southern hamburgers and hot dogs."

Hap Alexander opened the restaurant in 1986 and won a big fan base. He it sold to Greg Culp in 1994, who had worked for Hap from the beginning. In 2016, Greg sold to Jamie Gobbel, who knows the business, having worked at Hap's for 11 years. He promises to follow Hap's and Greg's footsteps. If he keeps Hap's the way it's made people so happy for so many years, he will earn the thanks of Wyndham Robertson, Randy Gardner, and the universe of Hap's fans.

FROM I-85 Take Exit 76 toward Salisbury and turn slightly left onto E. Innes St. Continue straight for about 0.5 mile before turning right on N. Main St., and Hap's will be on your left.

AFTER EATING Visit the beautifully restored railroad station a couple of blocks away at 215 Depot St.

Backcountry Barbeque

4014 Linwood-Southmont Road, Linwood, NC 27299
(336) 956-1696
Open every day 11:00 A.M.–9:00 P.M.

Backcountry is our last Lexington-area barbecue stop if you are going south on I-85, and the first if you are headed north. First or last, it is a good stop to make. There is a big woodpile in the back, and pork shoulders are cooking all the time.

My friend Grant McRorie told me that Backcountry might look bad on the outside, but the barbecue on the inside was mighty good. He was right on both counts.

Doug Cook, the owner, has done so well that he is able to spend most of his time in Colorado these days writing and performing music. But he has assembled a capable crew led by his stepdaughter, Christy Hunt, to cook and prepare the barbecue every day. One of the crew showed me how the pork is cooked all day over coals, and then kept warm with the help of electric cookers overnight to keep the barbecue from being too moist. Then I saw how they pull the fresh cooked meat from the bone and rough chop it just after the customer places an order.

All in all, a visit here is worth the little extra effort it takes to find it.

FROM I-85 Take Exit 88 (Linwood). (Be careful, and don't get confused—the road names and addresses are a jumble, but it is close to the intersection, and you can find it.) From the intersection, head east on NC 47 toward Linwood. Go about 0.8 mile. Backcountry Barbeque is on the right, across the road from a former furniture manufacturing plant.

Lexington Barbecue, Lexington

100 Smokehouse Lane, Lexington, NC 27295 · (336) 249-9814
Monday–Saturday 10:00 A.M.–9:30 P.M.; closed Sunday (and most
"Monday holidays" and for a week around July 4)

Lexington Barbecue is always busy and crowded. You will find locals and people from all over the state and beyond in line at mealtimes. But they never have to wait long—and they never feel rushed to finish. Owner Wayne Monk has a formula that gets food to the table quickly and keeps his customers happy.

I usually get a chopped tray with slaw, hushpuppies, and sweet iced tea. The food is very good, but what keeps me coming back is the way the waitresses take such good care of me—filling up my tea, getting more hushpuppies, smiling, and sometimes slipping and calling me "hon." "Need anything else, hon?" they ask.

I have been there so many times that I think Wayne Monk recognizes me when I come in. But even when I first started eating there and nobody knew me, they still treated me like I was part of the family.

When I leave, I am a few dollars poorer and feel a million dollars better. I think I would feel that way even if the food were not so good. But the barbecue, slaw, and hushpuppies are judged by the experts to be outstanding.

According to Jack Betts, former *Charlotte Observer* associate editor, Lexington Barbecue is "regarded by many travelers as the Mother Church of N.C. barbecue."

Bob Garner, author of *North Carolina Barbecue: Flavored by Time*, also uses religious terms to describe this place: "To the faithful, all roads still lead to Lexington Barbecue."

Barbecue insiders often refer to the restaurant and to Wayne Monk as "Honeymonk." I always wondered where such a name came from. Wayne explained that when he decided to open his own place, he borrowed $500 and got his brother-in-law, Sonny Honeycutt, to invest more and become an equal partner. Sonny had a sign made combining the two names, "Honeymonk's."

Ricky Byrd of Lexington Barbecue in Lexington

Wayne says he never approved, and the sign is now long gone, because Sonny quickly had enough of the barbecue business and left after 3 months.

In 2015, *USA Today* included Lexington Barbecue in their list of "Ten Best Southern Barbecue Spots." So even if you have never eaten here, it should be your first stop, even though it is several miles from I-85.

FROM I-85 *If headed north*: Take Exit 87 onto I-85 Business. Go 1.2 miles and take the second exit from the right lane onto US 64 West toward Mocksville. Go 0.1 mile and turn left onto W. Center St. Go 0.1 mile and turn left onto W. Center St. Ext. Go 0.2 mile and turn left onto Smokehouse Ln. Lexington Barbecue will be on the right.

If headed south: Take Exit 96 for US 64 toward Lexington/Asheboro. Turn right onto US 64. Go 5.2 miles and make a very sharp right onto Smokehouse Ln. Lexington Barbecue will be on the left. (Watch out! The turn onto Smokehouse Ln. is tricky and not even noted by some map services. Keep a lookout on the right. Just before the turn you will pass a park and then cross an overpass, which is just before the right turn onto Smokehouse Ln.)

AFTER EATING Walk around the side of the restaurant to get a look at the chimneys rising above the pit and, if you are lucky, get a whiff of the flavored smoke that comes out when the pork shoulders are cooking. If you have the courage, ask Rick Monk or another family member to show you the inside of the pit.

. . . .

Bar-B-Q Center

900 N. Main Street, Lexington, NC 27292 · (336) 248-4633
Monday–Saturday 6:00 A.M.–9:30 P.M.; closed Sunday

Lots of people thought Sonny Conrad's wood-cooked pork was the best they have ever had. When he died in July 2013, Sharon Myers wrote in the *Lexington Dispatch* that his "influence has effortlessly spread throughout the community from the tireless work ethic he showed through example to the one-on-one relationships he built with his customers and his role as a pioneer of the largest one-day festival in North Carolina, the Barbecue Festival."

With the founder of the restaurant gone, some people worried about its future. But the family and especially his wife, Nancy, and their two sons, Cecil and Michael, had been working in the business most of their lives. The family is continuing Sonny's traditions.

If you are willing to get a little farther off the main roads and make your way to downtown Lexington, you ought to try the food at Bar-B-Q Center. Some people rate the Conrads' wood-cooked pork as the best around.

You don't think about barbecue and ice cream making a good mix. But here they do. The restaurant started as a dairy bar, and you can still get a banana split or other ice cream treats to go with your barbecue.

FROM I-85 Take Exit 96 toward US 64/Lexington/Asheboro and go 4 miles. Then keep left onto N. Main St. (US 29-BR/US 70-BR) toward Lexington/Downtown. Go 0.4 mile. Bar-B-Q Center is on the right.

AFTER EATING Follow Main St. to downtown and visit some of the stores, like the Army-Navy Store at 14 N. Main St. Note that it features new specialty clothing and does not sell military surplus.

· ·

Southern Lunch

26 S. Railroad Street, Lexington, NC 27292 · (336) 248-5276
Tuesday–Friday 7:00 A.M.–8:00 P.M.;
Saturday 7:00 A.M.–12:00 P.M. (breakfast only);
closed Sunday–Monday

I was looking for a regular home-style restaurant in this barbecue town, and former Davidson County Board of Commissioners chairman Tommy Hedrick told me about Southern Lunch being a favorite of his because "everybody goes." Tommy loves the stew beef and scalloped tomatoes. Jack Briggs, owner of several funeral homes in the region, is a regular at lunch to get his favorites, which he says are "lima beans, scalloped tomatoes, and sweet potatoes."

Others praise the breakfast offerings and the chicken and dumplings, country-fried steak, sweet potatoes, meat loaf, and chicken pot pie.

Tommy Hedrick likes the friendly waitresses, the downtown location, and its owner, Herb Lohr. Herb is the third-generation owner of the business, started in 1925 near the old railroad depot. When I asked Lohr who would take over when he retired, he said, "I'm not thinking about that. I am going to be here until I die, just like my dad and my granddad. Most people don't have the opportunity to do what they were meant to do. My life has been great." Lohr gives his wife, Windy, and his love of sports credit for his happiness.

I asked Lohr why, in Lexington, the home of barbecue, there was no mention of it on his menu. His answer came quickly: "My grand-dad said, 'Everybody else has barbecue. I am not going to have it.'"

FROM I-85 Take Exit 94 and follow Old US 64 (Old Raleigh Rd.) toward Lexington. In about 0.5 mile bear left onto E. Center St. Ext. Follow E. Center St. Ext. and E. Center St. for about 3.5 miles to S. Railroad St. Turn left on S. Railroad St., and Southern Lunch will be on the right.

AFTER EATING Be sure to see the giant mural in the restaurant. It depicts life in downtown Lexington as it was in 1925 when the railroad was king. Then check out some of the special downtown retailers, like Conrad & Hinkle Food Market a few blocks away at 6 N. Main St. Established in 1919 by W. E. Conrad and E. Odell Hinkle, it has grown into one of the state's most respected spe-cialty food stores. People come from miles away to buy the special pimento cheese, made with American cheese rather than cheddar. At 2 S. Main St. is the Davidson County Historical Museum in the old 1856 courthouse, which was modeled on the Virginia state capitol.

On your way back to I-85, visit the Bob Timberlake Gallery at 1714 E. Center St. Ext.

Pioneer Family Restaurant and Steakhouse

10914 N. Main Street, Archdale, NC 27263 · (336) 861-6247
Monday–Thursday 11:00 A.M.–9:00 P.M.;
Friday 11:00 A.M.–9:30 P.M.; Saturday 7:00 A.M.–9:30 P.M.;
Sunday 7:00 A.M.–9:00 P.M.

The Pioneer Family Restaurant and Steakhouse has built a long-standing tradition of providing a full plate of country cooking and a great community gathering place. It's almost always packed with locals. You can order from a menu of charbroiled steaks, seafood, and sandwiches, but almost everybody goes to the 80-item buffet bar for a near-unlimited selection. It is a bargain in the evenings and on Sunday, and an even better deal at lunch from 11:00 A.M. to 3:00 P.M. on weekdays and Saturday.

My old friend the late Johnny Bailey lived nearby. He and his wife went several times a week. "Why so often?" I asked him "Well, I guess it's because we're gluttons," he said before he could think. "No don't print that. My wife will kill me."

Lots of people say that the buffet at the Pioneer is worth dying for. In 1987, Mike Liner and a partner opened Pioneer, eventually building the restaurant into a community institution. In 1993, then-congressman Howard Coble visited as part of a free luncheon for seniors. In the *Congressional Record* he reported that Mike gave "a place mat to each arriving senior citizen containing the seven rules which had to be followed in order to obtain a free meal. Those rules were: (1) No swinging from the chandeliers; (2) No dancing on tables; (3) No spitting tobacco juice on the floor; (4) No fistfights; (5) No food fights; (6) Police will be called for violators of the above rules; (7) Enjoy yourself. I can attest that all the rules, particularly No. 7, were observed with delight."

Mike sold the Pioneer in 1997 and ended up buying it back in 2009, after the owner decided to close up shop. Mike and his wife,

Kathy, came back as owners, bringing their daughter, Misty Austin, to help them manage. Kathy passed away in 2013, and her portrait and a loving tribute are on display as a reminder of how she helped build, and then rebuild, the Pioneer tradition.

Mike's advice for others going into business: "Do something you love and don't do it for the money." Sounds right to me.

FROM I-85 Take Exit 111 (High Point/Archdale). From the intersection, head west on NC 311 (Main St.) toward High Point. Go about 1 mile. The Pioneer Family Restaurant and Steakhouse is on the right.

· ·

Mary B's Southern Kitchen

3529 Archdale Road, Archdale, NC 27263 · (336) 861-5964
Monday–Friday 11:30 A.M.–2:30 P.M.; closed Saturday–Sunday

Mary Bunn started the restaurant in 1987. She sold it to Janet Thomas, who, with her husband, Alvin, has been running Mary B's since 1992.

"Just for lunch," she says. "And only on weekdays."

She continues, "We serve traditional southern food the way you remember it. This is the comfort food you grew up with. We don't believe in cutting corners here. If we wouldn't serve it to our family, we figure it's not good enough to serve to you. Come in, grab a chair, and you'll be a regular before you know it!"

Alvin says Janet's chicken pot pie, cooked the Moravian way without vegetables, is his and the customers' favorite. But Laura Cromer told me she comes in at least once a week just for the meat loaf. Regular customer Mark Rumley swears by the fried chicken.

The food is served cafeteria-style, which appeals to customers in a hurry. But most visitors prefer to linger and enjoy Janet's and Alvin's warm hospitality.

FROM I-85 Take Exit 111 (High Point/Archdale). From the intersection, head west on NC 311 (Main St.) toward High Point. Go about 1 mile. Turn left on NC 62. Go about 0.5 mile. Turn left onto Archdale Rd. Mary B's will be on the left in a small shopping center.

AFTER EATING One block away, on Trindale Rd., there are a couple of consignment shops that are worth a look.

. . . .

Kepley's Bar-B-Q

1304 N. Main Street, High Point, NC 27262 · (336) 884-1021
Monday–Saturday 8:30 A.M.–8:30 P.M.; closed Sunday
kepleysbarbecue.com

Is Kepley's worth a side trip from the interstate? You will get a definite "yes" from almost everybody who grew up in High Point, where Kepley's is a community institution that brings back many happy memories. Kepley's is plain and simple, just like it has been since 1948 when it opened. That might be the secret of its success. Or maybe it is their special vinegar-based and pepper-flavored barbecue that has kept people coming back for almost 70 years.

Chapel Hill lawyer Bob Epting grew up in High Point. He says Kepley's barbecue sandwich makes his mouth and his heart "fly back 50 years, to our '57 Chevys and Fords. Kepley's vinegar-based barbeque and slaw are just that unique. I guarantee you will never have had a better barbeque treat, certainly not one that works its magic in your memory, taking you home again to memories of hurried conversations with pals about which girl you wished you had the courage to call, and their long lost but still familiar faces."

After those lovely memories, how could anyone not stop by to experience Kepley's?

In 1948, Hayden Kepley started selling barbecue in an old army Quonset hut. In 1962, Kepley retired and sold Kepley's Bar-B-Q to his son-in-law, Charlie Johnson, and Bob Burleson, who had worked as a curb boy since he was 16. They worked together for many years, and now Burleson and his daughter, Susan, are the owners.

FROM I-85 *If headed north*: Take Exit 111 onto Main St./US 311 South toward High Point and go 6 miles. Kepley's is just before Main intersects Lexington Ave.

If headed south: Take Exit 118 and follow I-85 Business toward High Point for 7 miles. Exit onto Main St. (US 311) and go toward High Point for 3 miles. Kepley's is just before Main intersects Lexington Ave.

AFTER EATING Bob Epting suggests a visit to High Point Central High School's building, just a shady 4-block walk. Completed in 1926 and designed by Greensboro architect Harry Barton in Collegiate Gothic style, it was considered the grandest educational building in the state.

Other eateries in the area, including Stamey's Barbecue, are described in the I-40 chapter.

. . . .

Jack's Barbecue

213 W. Main Street, Gibsonville, NC 27249 · (336) 449-6347
Monday–Saturday 11:00 A.M.–7:00 P.M. (closing early on
Wednesday and Saturday); closed Sunday

Jack's is small and a little bit out of the way. But the folks are so nice, and downtown Gibsonville is a wonderful slice of small-town North Carolina.

The food is good, too. They like to brag about their special, Jack's Big Boy, a giant burger with lettuce, tomatoes, onions, mayonnaise, mustard, and melted cheese. If it sounds like something you could get at a fast food place, believe me when I say that it really tastes quite different, quite wonderful—just like the hamburgers at your favorite place back home.

In 1967, Jack Rook bought Henry's Barbecue, where he had been working. He changed the name to Jack's, which moved to its current location in 1970. Jack's daughter Kathy Sykes is the owner. Another daughter, Jacki Allison, is manager.

Jack's Barbecue in Gibsonville

If you're lucky, famous Gibsonville natives like former NC State and NFL football player Torry Holt could drop by. Another native, the late NC State women's basketball coach Kay Yow, was a regular when she came back home. Check out the displays about Holt, Yow, and other Gibsonville heroes.

FROM I-85 Take Exit 138. Head north on NC 61. Go about 3 miles to where this road intersects with W. Main St. in downtown Gibsonville. Turn right on W. Main, and Jack's is on the right.

AFTER EATING Spend some time on Main St., including a visit to Wade's Jewelers, located at 101 E. Main St. in a palatial building, inside and out. Stop by Once upon a Chocolate at 139 Piedmont Ave. to see an unbelievable display of chocolates made on-site. At 137 Piedmont Ave. is Pete's Grill, another favorite local eatery.

Hursey's Pig-Pickin' Bar-B-Q

1834 S. Church Street, Burlington, NC 27215 · (336) 226-1694
Monday–Saturday 11:00 A.M.–9:00 P.M.; closed Sunday

I would stop at Hursey's just for the great smells of burning hickory wood coming out of its chimneys all day long. Inside, I like to look at the gallery of people who have told Charlie Hursey that his barbecue is among the "best": Presidents Reagan, Clinton, and the first Bush, Senator Helms, and Governor Hunt. Hursey says he usually votes Republican in presidential races, but he is proud to serve presidents and politicians of all parties.

Hursey's can trace its beginnings to 1945 when Sylvester Hursey and his wife, Daisy, began combining a special sauce with his father's method of cooking pork.

Charlie got his start working for his parents as a carhop. He joined the business full time in 1960.

Hursey's is home to a big take-out business. There is also a small, comfortable seating area. The menu is limited to barbecue and fried seafood. Hursey's fans, like the *Charlotte Observer*'s Jack Betts, swear that Hursey's is one of the best barbecue stops in the state.

In my book, Hursey's wins the hushpuppy contest, with its fresh, golden, crispy cakes that are sweet enough to be dessert.

FROM I-85 Take Exit 143. Head north on NC 62 (Alamance Rd.). Go about 1 mile to where this road intersects with NC 70 (Church St.). Hursey's is on the left at this intersection.

AFTER EATING The Alamance County Historical Museum is located on part of a 1,693-acre grain plantation, known in the nineteenth century as Oak Grove. The plantation was owned by three generations of the Holt family, pioneers in the textile business as early as 1837. Follow NC 62 south for about 5 miles to 4777 NC 62. Call ahead before visiting at (336) 226-8254.

Sutton's at the Wrike, Graham

114 N. Main Street, Graham, NC 27253 · (336) 350-7293
Monday 7:00 A.M.–4:00 P.M.;
Tuesday–Saturday 7:00 A.M.–7:00 P.M.;
Sunday 9:00 A.M.–4:00 P.M.

Located in a former Wrike's Pharmacy building, Sutton's at the Wrike brings a branch of Chapel Hill's famed Sutton's Drug Store to Graham. Because Sutton's in Chapel Hill is a place I like to hang out—and have for many years—I feel at home in Sutton's at the Wrike. Just like in Chapel Hill, Sutton's at the Wrike serves breakfast, hot dogs, hamburgers, and diner food and a selection of more than 100 classic bottles of soda, along with an assortment of candy and jams. (I describe the Chapel Hill Sutton's in the I-40 chapter.)

Don Pinney, the owner of Sutton's in Chapel Hill, and his son, Clay, fell in love with Graham and its classic downtown, and when the Wrike's building became available they saw the opportunity to grow. Clay manages the Graham location. From every report, Clay has brought the same friendly and responsive service to the people of Graham.

My favorite Sutton's breakfast is the #3 with eggs over easy with biscuit, a heap of bacon, and grits. For lunch, nothing beats the Sutton's hamburger. If you're in Chapel Hill or just passing through Graham, nothing beats a good sit-down lunch at Sutton's.

FROM I-85 Take Exit 147 for NC 87 North. Then turn left onto NC 87 North/S. Main St. In less than a mile, at the traffic circle take the second exit onto N. Main St., and Sutton's will be on the left.

AFTER EATING Wander around the compact downtown Graham, and take a look at its classic courthouse. Walk a few blocks to inspect two historic houses across Main St.: first, the Williamson House, at 141 S. Main St., built about 1878 and restored for use by Bank of America; second, the Captain James White home, 213 S. Main St., built about 1873 and currently occupied by Alamance

Arts, the local arts council, which provides a venue for the changing exhibitions and a location for Picasso's Gift Shop.

. . . .

Village Diner

600 W. King Street, Hillsborough, NC 27278 · (919) 245-8915
Wednesday–Saturday 7:00 A.M.–2:30 P.M. and 5:00 P.M.–9:00 P.M.;
Sunday 7:00 A.M.–2:30 P.M.; closed Monday
villagedinernc.com

The Village Diner has a long history in Hillsborough. In 1975, Raymond Stansbury and his wife, Ethel, opened a restaurant in the front yard of his family's home, located about a mile from the center of Hillsborough. After Raymond died, Ethel, along with her daughter, Teresa Cox, continued serving southern county cooking and barbecue at modest prices. The diner was the town's oldest continuously operating restaurant. The generous portions (all-you-could-eat) made it one of Hillsborough's most popular places to gather and eat.

Then, in 2015 it closed. Lots of us were still in mourning when we learned that it was open again. The new owner, Joel Bohlin, told the *News of Orange* that he took pride in his food and planned to expand the menu. "Comfort food deserves quality," Bohlin said. "What we serve, we want to take pride in it."

Bohlin has kept his word and is serving good comfort food with a variety of options. He is connecting with local farmers to help source their ingredients. Though the buffet is no more, Bohlin has given the Village Diner a new lease on life, much to the delight of all of us.

FROM I-85 Head east on I-40 East/I-85 North. Take Exit 161 for US 70 East toward NC 86 North. Turn left onto US 70 Connector North. Then merge onto US 70 East. Turn right onto W. Hill Ave. North and turn left onto W. King St. The Village Diner will be on the left.

AFTER EATING Check out the downtown and experience local history at every corner.

Hillsborough BBQ Company

236 S. Nash Street, Hillsborough, NC 27278 · (919) 732-4647
Tuesday–Saturday 11:30 A.M.–9:00 P.M.;
Sunday 11:30 A.M.–8:00 P.M.; closed Monday
hillsboroughbbq.com

Hillsborough BBQ Company is not a longtime, family-owned operation like almost every other restaurant in this collection. But it has
something that only a few barbecue restaurants have: a real old-time
pit where they cook pork butts over wood coals made from hand-
picked hickory and oak. The management-ownership team assembled by Tommy Stann has local folks singing praises. For instance,
my dentist, Sam Nesbit, who lives in Hillsborough, is a big fan and
says he's never been disappointed. In addition to enjoying the good
food, he says, "if tables are full, or if you happen to be by yourself,
there is always a TV in the corner and a congenial crowd at the bar."

Former UNC–Chapel Hill provost Jim Dean and his wife, Jan,
were big fans of local home cooking, and although they now live in
New Hampshire, where Jim is president of the University of New
Hampshire, they still put Hillsborough BBQ at the top of their list of
favorites. Lee Smith, North Carolina's beloved author and a former
owner of Akai Hana, a wonderful Japanese restaurant in Carrboro,
tells me she eats at Hillsborough BBQ at least three times a week.

FROM I-85 Take Exit 164 and follow S. Churton St. for 1.5 miles.
Turn left onto W. Margaret St. Go 1 mile. Turn left on S. Nash.
Go 1 block.

AFTER EATING Walk 2 blocks on Calvin St. to the entrance to
Hillsborough's River Walk, which runs through the town and con-
nects to the Mountains-to-Sea Trail. Use it to go for a short walk
or bike ride along the Eno River.

Joel Bohlin and Tommy Stann of Hillsborough BBQ Company in Hillsborough

Bennett Pointe Grill & Bar

4625 Hillsborough Road, Durham, NC 27705 · (919) 382-9431
Monday–Friday 11:30 A.M.–2:30 P.M. and 5:00 P.M.–9:30 P.M.;
Saturday 5:00 P.M.–9:30 P.M.; Sunday 12:00 P.M.–8:00 P.M.

"We are so lucky. We just pray that it will never close," Janet Wells told me when I interrupted her quiet lunch with her sister at the Bennett Pointe Grill & Bar. "We live nearby, so we come here often. It is like home." Her 90-plus-year-old mother comes often, too, and always orders her favorite, chicken salad.

Friendly, longtime employees like Roslyn Evans (13 years) and Ashley Sealy (16 years) told me they enjoy getting to know their customers.

Bennett Pointe might be a little bit more upscale in décor and price than the usual neighborhood eatery, but it has found a formula that virtually guarantees a good experience for regulars like Janet Wells and visitors like me.

In 1997, when Lisa and Jonathan Lark first opened their restaurant, it had only 60 seats. Since then it has expanded and seats 160, including a full-service bar. The menu, at both lunch and supper, is varied, with soups, salads, and sandwiches, and entrées of meats and seafood are available along with daily specials.

FROM I-85 *If headed north*: Take Exit 170 and follow US 70 Business for about 2 miles. Bennett Pointe will be on the right, next door to Food Lion in a shopping center.

If headed south: Take Exit 173 (Cole Mill Rd.) and follow Cole Mill Rd. for 0.3 miles. Then turn right onto Hillsborough Rd. (US 15-501) and go about 2 miles. Bennett Pointe will be on the left, next door to Food Lion in a shopping center.

AFTER EATING Visit Bennett Place Historic Site, where the largest troop surrender of the American Civil War took place. It is just a short walk or drive from the restaurant along Bennett Place Memorial Dr., which runs behind the shopping center. In the simple farmhouse, Confederate general Joseph E. Johnston and Union general William T. Sherman negotiated for several days and, on April 26, 1865, signed a surrender agreement like the one signed more than 2 weeks earlier at Appomattox.

· ·

Bullock's Bar-B-Cue

3330 Quebec Drive, Durham, NC 27705 · (919) 383-3211
Tuesday–Saturday 11:30 A.M.–8:30 P.M.;
closed Sunday–Monday
bullocks-bbq.com

Bullock's may be the oldest continuously operating restaurant in Durham. It's where I got the idea to write this very book.

I was hungry, not just hungry for anything, but hungry for home cooking. In that city, I knew what to do—I headed for Bullock's. The lunchtime rush was long over, but it was still full. After I got settled in a booth, the waitress came up from behind me. I could hear her smiling as she said, "How you doing, hon?"

I had never seen the woman before, but she called me "hon."

For just a second I was the happiest man in the world. I knew that this woman, Sue Clements, was going to bring me a glass of sweet tea and keep it full the whole time I was there. She was going to treat me like we had been good friends forever.

Happy as I was, I started worrying about all those other people driving up and down I-40 and I-85, just a few miles away. Some of them, I thought, are just as hungry for a home-style meal as I am. They would love to be called "hon" and have their tea glasses kept full by Sue Clements. I knew I should seek out and share Bullock's and other home-cooking places with you and others.

If somebody like Sue Clements keeps your glass filled with sweet tea, what more do you need to say about Bullock's? But some of Bullock's fans will insist on telling you, "Everybody in Durham goes there."

It's true. A few minutes after Sue Clements filled my glass a second time, Susan Hester and Tonia Butler came in for a late lunch. We had worked together while I was on an interim assignment at North Carolina Central University.

They sensed that I was surprised to see them. "But D. G., didn't you know we always come to Bullock's?" Susan asked. "We come here all the time."

"I came to get me some fresh vegetables because I need something healthy," said Tonia Butler. But when she saw my barbecue, fried chicken, Brunswick stew, slaw, hushpuppies, and sweet tea, she laughed and told Sue Clements, "Same as he got."

She told me, "The healthy stuff will just have to wait."

Celebrities come here, too. Susan told me, "Shirley Caesar," the gospel singer and minister, "eats here all the time." On the way out, I saw a whole wall full of photos of famous people who ate at Bullock's.

But none could have eaten much happier than I did.

Glen Bullock started cooking barbecue for friends in the 1940s and opened Bullock's in 1952. His son, the late Tommy Bullock, and his family have owned and operated the business since 1965, at its current location since 1970.

FROM I-85 *If headed north*: Take Exit 173. Turn right onto Cole Mill Rd. Go 0.2 mile. Turn left on Hillsborough Rd. Go 0.6 mile to LaSalle St. Turn left. (You will see a big Walgreen's on the corner.) Go one block to Quebec St. Bullock's is on the right.

If headed south: Take Exit 174B (you will exit to the left) and then be prepared for the Hillsborough Rd. exit, which comes up immediately on the right. Turn left on Hillsborough Rd. Go 0.6 mile to LaSalle St. on the left. Turn left here. (You will see a big Walgreen's on the corner.) Go 1 block to Quebec St. Bullock's is on the right.

AFTER EATING Duke University's campus, which includes the chapel, the Nasher Museum of Art, and the Sarah P. Duke Gardens, is so close. But if you have just a few minutes, drive through the East Campus site of Trinity College. It is only 2 miles from Bullock's along Hillsborough Rd. and Main St.

....

Skipper Forsyth's Bar-B-Q

2362 N. Garnett Street, Henderson, NC 27537 · (252) 438-5228
Monday–Thursday 10:00 A.M.–7:30 P.M.;
Friday–Saturday 10:00 A.M.–8:30 P.M.;
Sunday 11:00 A.M.–3:00 P.M.
skipperforsythsbbq.com

Skipper Forsyth opened his restaurant in 1946, and he still watches over it. Well, his portrait takes up a prominent place overlooking the current owner, Regina Ellis, Skipper's granddaughter, as she runs the restaurant. Skipper's remains popular with locals, especially at lunchtime, according to Dorothy Pierce. "Especially at lunch," she told me, "we get big crowds."

Barbecue is a big draw, but the combination plate that adds Brunswick stew and fried chicken with vegetables could make for a great goodbye feast for a traveler headed north.

I almost ordered the less-expensive child's plate when I saw that it included "10 and under only or 65 and older."

One of U.S. Representative George Holding's friends told me that he gets a call whenever the congressman is coming to Henderson, saying, "Let's eat at Skipper Forsyth's."

FROM I-85 Take Exit 217 toward Henderson onto Satterwhite Point Rd. (NC 1319). Go 1 mile and turn right onto US 158 East (N. Garrett St.). Go 0.2 mile. Skipper Forsyth's will be on the left.

AFTER EATING Visit the site of Henderson High School (now Henderson Middle School), where television personality Charlie Rose was a star basketball player. It is in downtown Henderson at 219 Charles St.

. . . .

220 Seafood

1812 N. Garnett Street, Henderson, NC 27536 · (252) 492-8084
Wednesday–Saturday 5:00 P.M.–9:30 P.M.;
Sunday 12:00 P.M.–2:30 P.M.; closed Monday–Tuesday

Though Henderson lost a legendary barbecue joint when Nunnery-Freeman Barbecue closed for good, there's still plenty of good eating for such a small town. 220 Seafood is one such standout. It's a local gathering spot, a place you can go to see what the locals eat. The lines are sometimes long, but they move fast. For those of us old enough to remember them, 220 will remind you of an old-fashioned fish camp. The specialty here is fried fish, and folks in Henderson recommend trout, croaker, and baby flounder with hushpuppies and coleslaw. They say it is always good and always plentiful.

Nancy Wykle, editor and publisher of *Henderson Daily Dispatch*, thinks the food at 220 Seafood is great. She likes it also because "it's a place where you get a pretty good cross-section of Henderson." She admires the restaurant even more because, on Mondays when it is closed to the public, it often partners with local nonprofits to host fundraisers.

FROM I-85 Take Exit 215 for US 158 East. Continue straight before turning left onto N. Garnett St., and soon after 220 Seafood will be on your right.

AFTER EATING Henderson is home to Raleigh Road Outdoor Theatre, built in 1949 and one of the few drive-in movie theaters still in business. Located at 3336 Raleigh Rd., it is across town from 220 Seafood but worth the trip if you have some good memories associated with family evenings at the drive-in in the 1950s.

. . . .

Whistle Stop Cafe

123 Hyco Street, Norlina, NC 27563 · (252) 456-0855
Monday–Friday 11:00 A.M.–8:00 P.M.; closed Saturday–Sunday
NO CREDIT CARDS

Norlina is a couple of miles off I-85, just south of the Virginia line, hence its name and slogan from the town's website: "Norlina, where North Carolina begins." So it's the last place to get North Carolina–style home cooking for northbound travelers and the first place to touch down on the way back home.

I asked for help in finding a good local eatery from Jennifer Harris, editor of the *Warren Record* in nearby Warrenton. She wrote, "There's a restaurant in Norlina called Whistle Stop Cafe that has been around awhile. Home cooking for lunch and dinner, closed on Sundays, locally owned and operated. They have daily specials (Thursday is chicken livers!), and my personal favorite menu item (which I get every time I go) is the country-fried steak with gravy and onions on my mashed taters, another side, and sweet tea, of course! They have some homemade desserts that change daily."

This was great news—just the kind of place I look for. I learned later that Jennifer's paper had awarded the Whistle Stop top honors for Warren County restaurants.

When I visited the Whistle Stop Cafe, Sheila Arnold, one of a team of cheerful, friendly women who work there, greeted me. Sheila brought me the Tuesday special: fried chicken. I got dark meat, which cost a little bit less than the $7.25 for white meat. Tea is $1.59. The special came with two vegetables.

When I bit into the crispy, juicy chicken, I knew I had come to the right place.

Sheila explained that the owner, Lisa Willis, was too busy in the kitchen to talk. But when Lisa's husband, Ebin, dropped by for lunch, he explained that she liked to stay in the kitchen, leaving the customer service aspects of the business to her carefully selected staff. A good meal, nice people, and a trip back in time.

But don't come without cash. They don't take credit cards. And note that Whistle Stop is closed on weekends.

FROM I-85 *If headed north*: Take Exit 226 and follow Ridgeway-Drewry Rd. toward Ridgeway for about 2.5 miles. Turn left on US 1/158 and go about 2 miles into Norlina. Turn right onto Hyco St. Whistle Stop is on the right.

If headed south: Take Exit 233 and follow US 1 for about 7 miles into Norlina. Turn left onto Hyco St. Whistle Stop is on the right.

AFTER EATING Is there anything else to do in Norlina? Sheila explained that the mayor could open up the railroad museum for me, but I found another gem a few doors away. The hardware store, owned and operated by Judy Hayes, gave me a great chance to experience the flavor of an old-time general store.

First, Hayes showed me bins and bins of all kinds of seeds. Then she demonstrated the micro scales she uses to weigh small amounts of seeds. "I will sell you a package for a couple of dollars," she said "but if you just want 35 cents' worth, I can measure that out for you."

Or, if you have a few extra minutes, you can visit the antique shop in the 1863 depot in the tiny community of Warren Plains, just 2 miles away. From Norlina, follow Warren Plains Rd., King Rd., to Cook's Chapel Rd. Call ahead to be sure it's open: (252) 432-7132. When TV personality Charlie Rose was a child, his father ran a store near the depot. Rose credits his experience working in the store when he was 8 years old for his interest in listening to other people. He told the *Savannah Morning News*, "I was a young kid and I wanted to have conversations with adults; you have to speak to their world. . . . You have to know who they are, what they're about, what their curiosity is, what their experience is, what they're good at. People like to talk. And people like to talk about themselves."

INTERSTATE **95**

I've updated *Roadside Eateries* to make sure you have the best information possible for finding those great places where you can eat like a local. Since our first book, there have been some ups and downs for folks along I-95, including storms and, well, just life itself. Flooding along the Lumber River from Hurricane Matthew knocked out Fuller's Old Fashioned Bar-B-Q in Lumberton. Thank goodness Fuller's in Fayetteville is still open and the family has opened a new Fuller's in nearby Pembroke. The flooding also contributed to the demise of Candy Sue's, a favorite of world-famous author and Lumberton native Jill McCorkle.

And sometimes restaurants just close because life happens. When Wilber's Barbecue, a Carolina classic, closed up in March of 2019, it was, to me, a shock. Wilber Shirley had been in business since 1962, when he bought Hill's Barbecue. He still cooked the old-fashioned way, over pits with wood coals and all night slowly, carefully cooking whole hogs. The real barbecue experts say this makes all the difference. In his classic book, *The Best Tar Heel Barbecue*, Jim Early opined, "The name Wilber's and Eastern North Carolina barbecue are synonymous."

Even through life changes and storms, I must have traveled along I-95 a hundred times. At every intersection, it seems, there is the same combination of gas stations, motels, and fast food places. But let me tell you a secret: you can pull off the interstate almost anywhere between Lumberton and Roanoke Rapids, drive a few

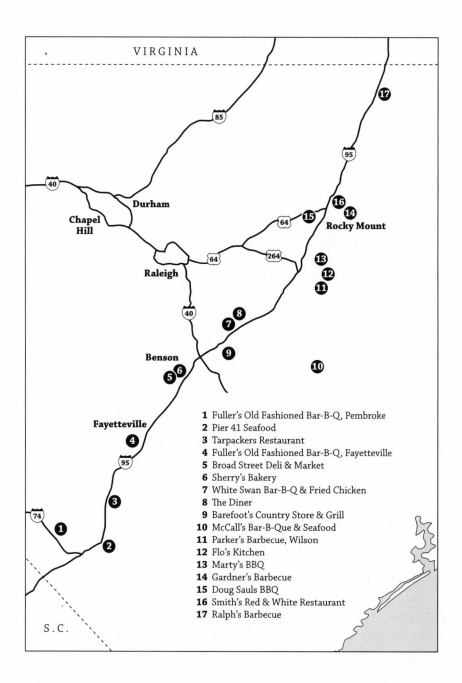

VIRGINIA

85

40

Durham

Chapel
Hill

64   15   16   14
Rocky Mount

Raleigh   64   264   13
                          12
                          11
40   8
       7

Benson   9
        6
      5   10

Fayetteville
        4
      95

      3

74
    1

    2

S.C.

1 Fuller's Old Fashioned Bar-B-Q, Pembroke
2 Pier 41 Seafood
3 Tarpackers Restaurant
4 Fuller's Old Fashioned Bar-B-Q, Fayetteville
5 Broad Street Deli & Market
6 Sherry's Bakery
7 White Swan Bar-B-Q & Fried Chicken
8 The Diner
9 Barefoot's Country Store & Grill
10 McCall's Bar-B-Que & Seafood
11 Parker's Barbecue, Wilson
12 Flo's Kitchen
13 Marty's BBQ
14 Gardner's Barbecue
15 Doug Sauls BBQ
16 Smith's Red & White Restaurant
17 Ralph's Barbecue

miles in any direction, and run into a local, family-owned restaurant. Its staff will be friendly, and the locals glad to see you.

But since you might not have time to do the exploring, I have gathered a group of possible stopping places that will give you the chance to dine at restaurants owned by members of the Lumbee Tribe, at several popular all-you-can-eat buffets, and at some highly praised Eastern-style barbecue restaurants.

If you like to eat a lot, you will love the way country cooking is usually served at some of the places along I-95. It is often buffet-style and sometimes "all you can eat." In fact, after you visit some of the places I am going to describe, I bet you will start calling I-95 "the Boulevard of Buffets."

Driving north on I-95 you will also run into some of North Carolina's best-known barbecue restaurants. I am not going to start taking sides about what kind of North Carolina barbecue—Eastern or Lexington—is better. But if you like the Eastern style, then driving up I-95 as you approach the Virginia line could be your pathway to paradise.

Unfortunately, most of us are afraid to take the extra few minutes to explore, instead rushing to some important meeting or hurrying home. And when we get hungry on I-95, we usually breeze through the drive-through, don't we? Then, later on, we kick ourselves for not being more adventurous.

But here's where I can help. I've found some places for you to visit. It will take you a few extra minutes, but I'm going to try to persuade you that the little bit of extra time will pay off with good food and good memories.

Fuller's Old Fashioned Bar-B-Q, Pembroke

100 E. Third Street, Pembroke, NC 28372 · (910) 521-4667
Monday–Tuesday 11:00 A.M.–9:00 P.M.;
Thursday–Saturday 11:00 A.M.–9:00 P.M.;
Sunday 11:00 A.M.–6:00 P.M.; closed Wednesday
fullersbbq.com/index.php

In the 1980s, Fuller Locklear, a member of the Lumbee Tribe, and his wife, Delora, opened a small restaurant near their home, serving fried chicken and seafood, southern-style vegetables, and barbecue. From these humble beginnings, Fuller's became a bustling and famous place to eat. Locklear built a reputation for his collards, which he grew himself and would not serve unless they were fresh and in season. You had to make sure to come in the fall or winter if you wanted those delicious greens. Fuller and Delora are gone now, but their children continue their parents' work. "My mom always said, 'If you're going to cook, cook with your heart,'" son Eric told the *Fayetteville Observer*. "Treat people like family, and feed them like family."

When I was working at UNC-Pembroke in 1999, Thomas Ross, emeritus geography professor at UNC-Pembroke, and Scott Bigelow, the university's public relations officer, told me about Fuller's, praising the delicious southern cooking and the variety on their buffet line. When my family and I stopped there early one Sunday afternoon, the restaurant was full with the after-church crowd.

After 30 years in business, along came Hurricane Matthew in 2016. The storm poured 8 feet of water into the restaurant, effectively destroying it. The Locklear family found rebuilding would be too difficult, and everyone assumed the restaurant was done for good. However, when Sheff's Seafood, one of my favorite restaurants in nearby Pembroke, closed, Fuller's moved into its location.

Scott Bigilow, writing for the *Robesonian* in Lumberton, captured the excitement of a Pembroke resident, who said, "Every day I drive by and can't help but think of those candied yams, rutabagas and corn bread. Just thinking of that long bar filled with all those scrumptious foods makes me hungry."

Indeed, just the sight of the buffet would set anybody off. Now, you can order a modest meal from Fuller's menu if you are not too hungry, but still the buffet is hard to resist. It has every kind of vegetable, a huge selection of meats, a giant salad bar, and as for desserts? Cobbler, pies, and soft ice cream are all available for your sweet tooth. All for a modest price.

My friend and former congressional staffer Don DeArmon lives in Maryland, but when his family is on the road to the NC coast, they like to stop at Fuller's. "They always have a fresh something, this time collards, and we like their deviled crab—even as I'm filling up on rice and black-eyed peas with a side of fresh corn. We also like the vibe. A very friendly mix of locals and travelers." DeArmon is not alone. *Southern Living* magazine named Fuller's one of the South's Top Five "Great Interstate Highway Barbecue Joints."

Now that they're settled into the old Sheff's Seafood spot, there's no time like the present to stop at Fuller's for some good company and good food.

FROM I-95 Turn right onto Owen Dr. and then right again onto Dallas St. In less than 0.5 mile, turn right onto Southern Ave. In about 1.5 miles turn left onto Gillespie St. After about 0.5 mile, turn right onto E. Russell St. In less than 1 mile turn left onto S. Eastern Blvd., and Fuller's will be on the left.

Pier 41 Seafood

2401 E. Elizabethtown Road, Lumberton, NC 28358 · (910) 738-8555
Wednesday–Saturday 11:00 A.M.–9:00 P.M.;
Sunday 11:00 A.M.–8:00 P.M.; closed Monday–Tuesday
pier41seafood.com

I'd heard from several trusted sources that there was a seafood joint called Pier 41 in Lumberton that rivaled those on the coast. I found it hard to believe myself, but if Pier 41 was really as good as the legendary seafood restaurants in Calabash, it would be well worth the extra couple of miles from Exit 20 across Lumberton on NC 211 to get there.

The verdict? It is well worth it. In fact, I would drive many extra hours for Pier 41's Calabash-style, lightly breaded fried fresh seafood. What's more, they heap the plate with generous portions, and their prices are very reasonable.

Owner Stephen Runkle worked his way into the food industry over many years by selling and distributing food products to restaurants in the region. He and his wife, Patty, have put together a team of fantastic cooks and servers whose friendliness complement their talents in preparing and serving their good food.

My favorites are the fried fresh fish, but there are a variety of other good offerings, such as broiled and boiled seafood, appetizers, a salad bar, and non-seafood items such as barbecue ribs.

FROM I-95 Take Exit 20 for NC 211 toward NC 41/Lumberton/Red Springs. Turn left onto NC 211 South/N. Roberts Ave. In less than 2 miles turn left onto E. Elizabethtown Rd. and Pier 41 will be on the left.

AFTER EATING If you are a fan of novelist and Lumberton native Jill McCorkle, explore her Lumberton hometown and the inspiration for her mythical town of Fulton. The cemetery in her novel *Life after Life* is modeled on Meadowbrook Cemetery. If you follow N. Roberts St. back to Exit 20, the cemetery will be on your left.

Turn left onto N. Walnut St. to get to the cemetery entrance. For a pleasant walk along the Lumber River, Riverwalk is accessible from W. Fifth St. It runs along the river from downtown to Luther Britt Park, a walk of approximately 1.5 miles from beginning to end, or a 3-mile round trip. It includes areas that overlook the river and is wonderful for bird watching.

....

Tarpackers Restaurant

201 W. Broad Street, Saint Pauls, NC 28384 · (910) 865-1560
Tuesday–Thursday and Sunday 11:00 A.M.–2:00 P.M.;
Friday (and second Saturday of each month) 4:30 P.M.–8:30 P.M.;
closed Monday and Saturday
tarpackers.com

The name "Tarpackers" comes, of course, from a combination of "Tar Heel" and "Wolfpack," two nicknames of our state's rival public universities. Tarpackers doesn't try to settle the argument about which school is better.

In October 2011, Phyllis Williams acquired Tarpackers from former owners Linwood and Sara Hayes. She continues to celebrate the history and tradition of both schools. She is a Tar Heel fan, and her husband, Bill, pulls for NC State. The food is simple, light, and reasonably priced.

FROM I-95 Take Exit 31 (NC 29/Saint Pauls). Head east on NC 20 (Broad St.) and go 1 mile. Tarpackers will be on your right.

Fuller's Old Fashioned Bar-B-Q, Fayetteville

113 N. Eastern Boulevard, Fayetteville, NC 28301 · (910) 484-5109
Monday–Saturday 11:00 A.M.–9:00 P.M.;
Sunday 11:00 A.M.–6:00 P.M.
Fullersbbq.com

If you missed Fuller's in Lumberton or can't wait until you get there
to eat, you are in luck. Fuller Locklear's children brought Fuller's to
the Fayetteville area with a buffet just like the original. Now, keep
in mind that we're talking about the location in Fayetteville proper,
but since the publication of the last edition of *Roadside Eateries*, a
new Fuller's outside the city on NC 401 has opened. Both locations
serve the same barbecue as the original Lumberton restaurant. It is
all cooked on the grounds of the Locklear homeplace, where Fuller
began more than 20 years ago (for their history, see the Fuller's
entry for Pembroke, above). Truly a barbecue empire in the making.

FROM I-95 Take Exit 52. Follow NC 24 west toward Fayetteville for
3 miles. Turn left onto N. Eastern Blvd. (I-95 Business/US 301) for
0.3 mile. Fuller's will be on your right.

AFTER EATING Only about 2 miles from Fuller's, via Grove St. and
Rowan St., is the world-class U.S. Army Airborne & Special Operations Museum, which honors and preserves the legendary feats of
the airborne and special operations troops. Wonderful, gripping
exhibits. Free admission.

Stephenson's Bar-B-Q and Meadow Village Restaurant,
other eateries in the area, are described in the I-40 chapter.

Broad Street Deli & Market

129 E. Broad Street, Dunn, NC 28334 · (910) 891-1002
Monday–Saturday 11:00 A.M.–3:00 P.M.; closed Sunday
broadstreetdeliandmarket.com

Broad Street Deli is not a typical meat-and-three diner, but it has become one of the favorite lunch spots in Dunn. Owners Jamie and Jeff Adkins take pride in their salads, soups, and sandwiches. Carroll Leggett, who grew up in Harnett County and is well known for his knowledge of North Carolina history, politics, and food, says, "Really an oasis. Upbeat with small wine shop, culinary treats to take on the road. Jamie Adkins, the owner, radiates warmth and the spot is a welcoming environment. Excellent chicken gumbo soup— one of my favorites—and hot ham and cheese on good bread."

Southern Living recently raved about Broad Street's pimento cheese. Co-owner Jamie plugs the signature sandwich called "The Life of Riley," full of roast beef and brie with plum sauce or mustard. It is named after Jamie and Jeff's son, Riley.

Every year Broad Street Deli hosts a reunion for the Dunn High School classes of 1961–64. Retired pharmacist Cliff Butler returns each year. He has a special connection to the deli's location. The building was the site of his father's drugstore, Butler and Carroll. Cliff says, "It still has the original floors that I mopped thousands of times as a teenager, and the soda fountain that was built into the store in 1927 is still there."

FROM I-95 Take Exit 73 for US 421/NC 55 toward Dunn/Clinton. Turn right onto E. Broad St. and go 1 mile. Broad Street Deli will be on the right.

AFTER EATING At 109 N. Wilson is LadyBugsInTheAttic for another selection of antiques and primitives. Walk along Broad St. and Wilson St. to get a feeling for a small-town downtown, and visit Sherry's Bakery (see below), where you can sample fresh pastries and cakes or just enjoy the aroma of baking bread.

Sherry's Bakery

122 N. Wilson Ave., Dunn, NC 28334 · (910) 892-3310
Monday–Saturday 6:00 A.M.–6:00 P.M.; closed Sunday
sherrysbakery.wixsite.com/sherrysbakery

Sherry's is another non-meat-and-three that has become a local hotspot. Dunn natives Cliff and Linda Butler recommend Sherry's. Cliff writes, "My standard order is two (sometimes three) hot dogs all the way with an order of fried okra. I never leave without a box full of the pastries. My favorite is the chocolate-covered, sugarcoated honey bun, which I drizzle with half & half and coat with a little butter before microwaving. This is a must try and well worth any fat or diabetes it may cause.

"Linda's dad was a member of the Wisdom Table, which meets every morning at Sherry's. It only takes one vote to become a member and you can vote for yourself. No subject is off limits and every world problem is solved by this group."

Owner Freddie Williford gave me a Wisdom Table membership card with the Rules and Benefits on the reverse side, requiring me "to be truthful most of the time." The bakery opened in 1945. Freddie and his wife, Mary, bought it in 1967 and named it after their six-year-old daughter. Today Sherry Williford Baysa and her brother, Fred, help manage Sherry's. Sadly, Mary died a few years ago. Freddie, born in 1932, is planning his retirement. "When I get to be 100 years old, I am going to hang it up—in 2032." In the meantime, every day Fred and his crew at Sherry's will be making and selling 75–100 dozen donuts, 55 pounds of chicken salad, and numerous pies, cakes, and other pastries.

FROM I-95 Take Exit 73 for US 421/NC 55 toward Dunn/Clinton. Turn right onto E. Broad St. and go 1 mile to N. Wilson Ave. Sherry's is on the right at the corner.

AFTER EATING Just a few blocks away at 209 W. Devine St. is the General William C. Lee House. It contains offices for the Dunn Area Chamber of Commerce and a museum memorial to the Dunn native who was a pioneer of U.S. airborne troops, first commander of the army's jump school at Fort Benning, commander of the then newly formed 101st Airborne Division, and a major planner for the D-Day airborne operations.

. . . .

White Swan Bar-B-Q & Fried Chicken

3198 S. Brightleaf Boulevard, Smithfield, NC 27577 · (919) 934-8913
Monday–Wednesday 10:30 A.M.–7:30 P.M.;
Thursday–Saturday 10:30 A.M.–8:30 P.M.;
Sunday 10:30 A.M.–5:00 P.M.

The White Swan in Smithfield is an old-time barbecue place, just like the roadhouses of days gone by. Linwood Parker owns and runs the White Swan, along with the adjoining motel and an accounting business, and is very active in the political life of Johnston County.

Parker's family has long owned White Swan, but before the Parkers took over, there was a different kind of business on the hill. Known as Flowers' Tavern, it was built in 1930 by Percy Flowers, who grew up in nearby Archers Lodge. Flowers was a legendary moonshiner who made much more money making and selling whiskey than he did at the tavern. In his book *Lost Flowers*, Perry Sullivan, Flowers's son, writes that by the 1950s Flowers "was a high-rolling whiskey millionaire." By then Flowers had long since sold the restaurant.

Later it was acquired by Linwood Parker and his parents. He says that it's a classic southern family business, with all generations of the Parker clan pitching in. "We've had four generations interested in the business," he says, "and we're proud of it. The essence of life in the South is small family farms and businesses. So we're proud to be a part of that heritage."

Bob Garner brags about White Swan's barbecue in *North Carolina Barbecue: Flavored by Time*. Barbecue is the specialty, but there is great fried chicken, Brunswick stew, and ribs.

The restaurant is cozy, and a lot of its business done at the counter, with folks streaming in to get an order to take out. When I sat down and placed my order of barbecue and slaw, my meal was delivered to the table in less than a minute, along with a helping of some of the best hushpuppies I ever ate.

FROM I-95 Take Exit 90. Head north on US 301. Go 2 miles (passing Holts Lake). White Swan is on the left.

AFTER EATING Ask Linwood Parker to talk to you about Percy Flowers or modern-day North Carolina politics.

···

The Diner

314 E. Market Street, Smithfield, NC 27577 · (919) 934-6644
Monday–Friday 6:30 A.M.–2:00 P.M.;
Saturday 6:30 A.M.–11:00 A.M.; closed Sunday

Every small county seat town needs a small diner near its courthouse, a place where the lawyers and court officials can meet. For many years Shirley's, a classic downtown-style diner, served Smithfield's locals until it closed, leaving a void. More than 10 years ago, Miami natives Larry and Amy Holt moved to North Carolina and came to the rescue by opening The Diner. It fills the bill for locals and gives visitors the chance to share a piece of small-town life at breakfast and lunch.

Larry and Amy have specials every weekday: meat and two vegetables for $6.95. The most popular days, they say, are Monday for Larry's special meat loaf and Friday for fried flounder.

The Diner in Smithfield

FROM I-95 Take Exit 95 to E. Market St. Go 1 mile. The Diner will be on the left.

AFTER EATING Visit the celebrated Ava Gardner Museum across the street. Walk down a few blocks to the Smithfield Neuse River Walk's entrance on S. Front St. Take a look at the courthouse. Stop in the library, the Johnston County Visitors Bureau, and the Johnston County Heritage Center for information and displays of local history, all within walking distance.

Barefoot's Country Store & Grill

3295 US 701 South, Four Oaks, NC 27524 · (919) 989-9190
Monday–Saturday 5:30 A.M.–9:00 P.M.;
Sunday 7:30 A.M.–7:00 P.M.

In parts of our fair state, restaurants are few and far between—it is a big state, after all—but when you find one, you've not just found a place to eat, you've found a piece of North Carolina's character. Sometimes it's a fish shack near the coast or a cozy breakfast nook in a cool valley in the mountains. Barefoot's is something else, a place from what feels like the long-ago past but is a good reminder that our lives in big cities and college towns aren't the only kind of lives being lived in the Tar Heel State. This modest gas station and grill is a beloved local haunt for folks in Four Oaks, one that has stood the test of time and still offers some classic southern sides like pickled beets and fried squash, along with fried shrimp burgers and chicken gizzards.

So go and soak in the atmosphere of a time that might be slipping away from us, of a country store where locals and travelers alike can gather, tuck into some serious southern food, and catch up on the day's events. Note that Barefoot's harkens back to the past so strongly it doesn't have a website—truly old-school.

FROM I-95 Take Exit 87 toward Four Oaks. After 0.25 mile, turn left onto Keen Rd. Go 2.5 miles, then turn right onto US 701; go a little over a mile, and Barefoot's will be on the left.

McCall's Bar-B-Que & Seafood

139 Millers Chapel Road, Goldsboro, NC 27534 · (919) 751-0072
Open every day 11:00 A.M.–9:00 P.M.
mccallsbbq.com

Although Goldsboro is a long detour off of I-95, the iconic Wilber's had to be suggested as a possible side trip. When it closed in 2019, the question was, is a detour to Goldsboro still worth recommending? The answer is yes. The must-visit place is McCall's Bar-B-Que & Seafood, which serves great Eastern-style barbecue that some folks in Goldsboro like even more that Wilber's—so you know it's good 'cue. Another reason McCall's is beloved in the community is the sheer variety of the menu, which includes some of the best fried chicken in the state and special meat-and-three plates for under $10.

In his book *The Best Tar Heel Barbecue*, Jim Early writes, "The barbecue chicken's crisp skin conceals a melt-in-your-mouth moist offering that's tender and pink to the bone with good smoke penetration. The chicken is done, but not overdone. It's a taste sensation."

When my Goldsboro friends Emily and David Weil took me to lunch there, I found a large and cheerful crowd enjoying a bountiful buffet with ribs, fried and baked chicken, shrimp, oysters, fish, and a variety of sides.

Some folks might remember a branch of McCall's that operated for a few years in Clayton, about 45 minutes northwest of Goldsboro. It was crowded and popular, but co-owners Worth Westbrook and Randy McCall closed it to concentrate on the Goldsboro operation, which is managed by Randy's son, Allen. McCall's has been serving up great food and good times for over 30 years, and by the looks of it, they're not anywhere close to being done.

FROM I-95 From US 13 South, make a slight right onto Genoa Rd. Turn left onto Pecan Rd., then turn right onto Arrington Bridge Rd. After 1.9 miles, continue straight onto NC 581/Bill Lane Blvd. Turn left onto NC 111 North. Continue straight onto Millers Chapel Rd., and then turn left.

AFTER EATING Consider a visit to Cliffs of the Neuse State Park, at 240 Park Entrance Rd. in Seven Springs, and a short walk on one of the trails along the river and a view of the impressive cliffs overlooking the Neuse River.

. . . .

Parker's Barbecue, Wilson

2514–2580 US 301, Wilson, NC 27893 · (252) 237-0972
Open every day 9:00 A.M.–8:00 P.M. (take-out open until 8:15 P.M.)
parkersbarbecuewilson.com

First of all, let's set the record straight. There is some discussion about Parker's—maybe even some controversy. It is mostly about two questions. The first is whether Parker's is too far away from I-95, and too confusing to find, to be considered close and convenient enough to interrupt a long-distance trip.

The other question has to do with whether Parker's mostly gas-cooked barbecue can meet the standards of the barbecue purist.

Having raised these questions, about which there will always be debate, I can say with certainty that Parker's is well worth a stop. Especially if you are hungry. Especially if you want to see a lot of local people enjoying the ceremonies of fellowship and eating large quantities of country-style food.

Even if you have questions about the distance or the gas, don't pass by Parker's at mealtime if you are anywhere close by.

Some barbecue experts simply overlook the gas controversy and make their judgments on the results. For instance, Jack Betts praised Parker's a few years ago, writing about the "authentic, slightly dry Eastern North Carolina barbecue, and corn sticks that remind you that they still do things the good old way at The Original Parker's."

Why does it still taste so good? Eric Lippard, one of the managers of Parker's, reminded me, "It is still pit-cooked barbecue, and there aren't enough trees in North Carolina to cook it all."

Some fans, including New York chef and North Carolina barbecue expert Elizabeth Karmel, praise Parker's for other reasons. Karmel wrote in the May 2015 issue of *Saveur* about Parker's fried chicken, "This is the best chicken I've ever had in my life. It was so good that, the first time I had it, I got up and asked the owner of the restaurant how he made it. They do it really simply, very old-fashioned. It's got the crispiest skin, not greasy at all, and the place feels straight out of the 1950s."

It goes back even further, back to 1946, when three brothers started Parker's. In 1986, Don Williams, who had been working at Parker's since 1963, became the owner. In 1996, Eric Lippard and Kevin Lamm joined him as partners and managers. One of them is almost always on-site, and they welcome questions from their customers.

Eric was greeting customers at the door and charmed former Wake County School Board chair Patti Head. She had driven from Raleigh to meet her sister, Cookie Cantwell, who lives in Wilmington. They said they chose Parker's as their meeting place "because it's an institution, and everybody is so friendly, like Eric."

FROM I-95 Take Exit 119A-119B to I-795 South (US 117-264) and follow I-795 South for 5 miles. Then take Exit 43A to US 301 North toward Wilson. Go 2 miles. Parker's is on the left.

AFTER EATING Ask Eric Lippard to tell you the secret of Parker's highly praised fried chicken. Make a quick visit to Barton College (formerly Atlantic Christian College) about 4 miles away at 400 Atlantic Christian College Dr.

Flo's Kitchen

1015 Goldsboro Street South, Wilson, NC · (252) 237-9146
Tuesday–Saturday 4:00 A.M.–12:00 P.M.; closed Sunday–Monday
CASH ONLY

Though Wilson, North Carolina, is known for its barbecue restaurants—including the much-missed Bill's—it also has another southern food staple down pat: biscuits.

The "cat's head" biscuits at Flo's Kitchen will make you happy if you follow two rules: bring cash and get there before noon.

Don't be surprised if there is a big crowd both inside and outside. The Saturday morning I visited there was a block-long traffic jam beginning at Flo's drive-through.

The inside was jam-packed, too. But it's their big breakfast biscuits, about the size of a cat's head, hence the name, and what's inside them that have cars lining up to order beginning at 4:00 A.M. These are dedicated biscuit lovers, and they know a good biscuit when they see one.

Flo's opened in 1990 as a partnership between Florence Williams and her daughter, Linda Brewer. Before she died, Florence, or "Flo," taught the biscuit makers her secret process. It involves making the biscuits using lard and forming them by hand. The bakers make the bottom first, add some cheese, and wrap the rest of the dough around the filling. Once they're fresh from the oven, you can get these biscuits stuffed with eggs and meats. A local favorite is pork tenderloin and steak with hoop cheese. Locals call the treat a "buffet on a biscuit." Indeed, after one of these big biscuits, you might skip lunch.

Linda's daughter and her niece are working in the business, assuring a good transition that will keep those "biscuit buffets" available for many years.

FROM I-95 Take Exit 107 for US 301 toward Kenly/Wilson. Turn right onto US 301 North (signs for Wilson/I-95 North/Kenly/Rocky Mt.) and continue for about 14 miles. Turn left onto Goldsboro St. South. Flo's will be on the right.

AFTER EATING Take a quick trip to downtown Wilson via Downing St. and Goldsboro St. and visit the Vollis Simpson Whirligig Park at 301 Goldsboro St. It features Simpson's whimsical moving machines that drew thousands of visitors to his farm. According to the park's website, it anchors an effort to draw visitors to Wilson, where "weathered brick tobacco warehouses, 'five & dime' stores and a Classical Revival courthouse share newly renovated street space and signage with today's boutique shoppes, regional business incubator and burgeoning arts community."

. . . .

Marty's BBQ

2643 Ward Boulevard, Wilson, NC 27893 · (252) 281-1709
Open every day 10:30 A.M.–9:00 P.M.
martysbbq.com

For people in Wilson it was like a death in the family when Bill's Barbecue and Chicken Restaurant suddenly closed in early 2019 after being in business for 56 years. Its founder, Bill Ellis, who died 2 years earlier, built a tiny hot dog stand with 26 seats into a booming 250-seat restaurant and a catering business that served events across Eastern North Carolina. Bill had mastered the art of barbecue, but he was also known for his fried chicken and fresh local vegetables.

All is not lost. After Bill's death his son Lawrence, who grew up learning the business from his dad, opened his own restaurant in an old convenience store. He named it after his deceased brother, Marty. Bringing more than 30 years of experience working with his dad, he has turned his new restaurant into a bustling business.

From his dad, Lawrence learned the art of efficiently managing crowds of cars and hungry people, somehow getting tasty Eastern North Carolina barbecue, fried chicken, and fixings on the table when the customer is ready.

Friends in Wilson tell me that Lawrence has recreated the Bill's experience for them. They say barbecue runs in the family. One said the barbecue at Marty's is even better than it was at Bill's.

One of Bill's longtime workers who now works at Marty's told me, "This is like Bill's was in the early days."

Prices are reasonable. A small barbecue plate or fried chicken dinner costs less than $6.

Okay, there is a downside. Marty's is crowded at mealtimes. Lots of people are driving up, ordering, and taking the barbecue, chicken, and vegetables home.

It might be a problem, but it's good evidence that the people in Wilson are getting over the loss of Bill's and finding the same good food at Marty's.

FROM I-95 Take Exit 121 for US 264 toward Wilson/Sims for 0.2 mile. Turn right onto Raleigh Road Pkwy. W. Turn left onto Forest Hills Rd. N.W., and then turn left onto Point Dr. N.W. Turn left, and Marty's will be on the left.

. . . .

Gardner's Barbecue

1331 N. Wesleyan Boulevard, Rocky Mount, NC 27804
(252) 446-2983
Sunday–Thursday 10:00 A.M.–9:00 P.M.;
Friday–Saturday 10:00 A.M.–9:30 P.M.;
buffet opens 11:00 A.M. every day
gardnerfoods.com

Judging from the long line of folks waiting to eat at Gardner's Barbecue the last time I was there, its reputation is still going strong. Inside, most customers were eating all they wanted, choosing either to go through a buffet line or to be served family-style at the table. As good and plentiful as the food is, there is more to Gardner's than just eating.

The lively red-and-white table coverings are just part of the reason it is so bright and cheerful. People there smile at each other—and at strangers. It honestly made me feel I was at a church supper rather than a restaurant.

When the cash register attendants were too busy counting money to talk to me, Gloria Davis, the assistant manager, took me under her wing and answered all my questions. She told me that her boss, Gerry Gardner, brother of former congressman and lieutenant governor Jim Gardner, maintains the long family association with this country restaurant. Since that visit, Gerry's sons, Jay and Jaime, have purchased the company from their father and completed a major remodeling, which they promise will not affect the restaurant's reputation. They say, "We appreciate our loyal customers who have supported us for over 40 years and we plan to continue offering the same great-tasting Eastern NC–style BBQ and down-home cooking for years to come."

FROM I-95 Take Exit 138 to merge onto US 64 East toward Rocky Mount. Go 3.8 miles and take Exit 468A for Wesleyan Blvd./US 301. Turn left on N. Wesleyan Blvd. Go 1.5 miles, and Gardner's will be on the right.

AFTER EATING Visit the campus of North Carolina Wesleyan University, about 3.5 miles north on Wesleyan Blvd.

Doug Sauls BBQ

813 Western Avenue, Nashville, NC 27856 · (252) 459-2310
Wednesday–Saturday 11:00 A.M.–8:00 P.M.; closed Sunday–Tuesday

Randy Gardner is a quiet barbecue and home-cooking expert who has never led me in the wrong direction, food-wise. I can take his recommendations to the bank. He recently told me he'd just been to Doug Sauls BBQ. "It is really good BBQ," he tells me. "Good sides, too, black-eyed peas, Brunswick stew, green beans, boiled potatoes, and of course, coleslaw."

I agree with him and others who praise the Eastern-style barbecue, fried chicken, and fried seafood as being among the best in the state.

The moist and tender chopped barbecue makes a great sand-wich. But it is hard to pass by the fried chicken, which some say is as good as the pork. And, of course, you can count on me to order whatever is on the daily special.

Doug Sauls learned the restaurant business working in Rocky Mount. He opened the restaurant that bears his name about 30 years ago, and the family has owned the restaurant ever since. His son Steve grew up working there and purchased it from his mother, Lila Butler, in 2007. With the help of his wife, Kim; and their daughters, Megan and Jessie; son, Jordan; and loyal staff, Steve is continuing the decades-old family tradition. And I couldn't be happier.

FROM I-95 Take Exit 127 and turn left onto NC 97 West. In 2.5 miles, turn right onto NC 1001/Old Bailey Hwy. In 8 miles, continue onto S. Alston St., then turn left onto W. Cross St. and continue onto W. Washington St. Continue onto Western Ave., and Doug Sauls BBQ will be on your left.

. . . .

Smith's Red & White Restaurant

3635 N. Halifax Road, Rocky Mount, NC 27804 · (252) 443-0418
Tuesday–Saturday 6:30 A.M.–2:00 P.M.; closed Sunday–Monday
smithsredandwhite.com/restaurant

Pat Ashley, who travels all over Eastern North Carolina working with our public schools, got my attention with her enthusiasm for this place. She wrote, "Smith's restaurant is a superior southern meat-and-vegetable breakfast and lunch spot beside Smith's Red and White grocery right off I-95 just north of Rocky Mount. The menu of meats and vegetables changes daily. Always three or four different meats: smothered pork chops, fried chicken, meat loaf, as well as rare items like backbones. They have the best squash and rutabagas I have ever eaten as well as cheese biscuits to die for. There is a small-order menu with things like oysters in addition to the meat-and-

Smith's Red & White Grocery in Rocky Mount

vegetable daily specials, which are served cafeteria-style. I always bring home a take-out meal because it is better than anywhere I have found for real, old-style but high-quality southern food from the 1950s."

Three generations of the Smith family have nurtured the food in Dortches (part of greater Rocky Mount) since 1954, when S. B. (Sherwood) Smith began a small grocery business in the corner of a nearby farm supply store. In 1964, he moved to a cinder block building and expanded the grocery business to include pork processing.

About this time, S. B.'s son, Bruce, joined the business, and in 1999, Bruce's son, Derrick, signed on. The expanded grocery operations have thrived, and in 2010 the Smiths added the restaurant to feed the many visitors and to take advantage of the grocery's supply of fresh vegetables and meats.

FROM I-95 Take Exit 141 and turn onto NC 43 (Dortches Blvd.) toward Rocky Mount. Go 0.3 mile and turn left onto N. Halifax Rd. Red & White will be on the right.

AFTER EATING Stop by the grocery next door. It is even better known than the restaurant. People travel from all over, coolers in tow, to load up on the great sausage and specialty items, especially during the holiday season, when the store is decked out in holiday cheer. The sausage makes a great present in any season. For sweets to take home, stop by Tastee Creations Bakery and ask Hazel Armstrong about her special sweet-potato bread. Across the parking lot is Exit 141 Collections, which has eclectic offerings. If you have more time, take a look at the Dortch House, built in Federal style about 1810 and listed on the National Register of Historic Places. It is at 4976 Dortches Blvd., "catty-cornered" across from Red & White but covered with woods and vines. It is not visible from the road and is so hidden that many of the locals don't even know it's there.

. . . .

Ralph's Barbecue

1400 Julian R. Allsbrook Highway, Weldon, NC 27890
(252) 536-2102
Open every day 9:00 A.M.–8:30 P.M.
ralphsbbq.com

You could argue all you want with Wes Woodruff, a Roanoke Rapids native who now lives in Orlando, Florida, but you are not likely to change his firm opinion that Eastern style is the "only kind of barbecue." Nor will you persuade him that Ralph's is not the best place in North Carolina to eat. Woodruff declares, "My wife and I usually get back to Roanoke Rapids twice a year or so, and Ralph's is a mandatory stop. We usually get several pounds of barbecue and several quarts of Brunswick stew, freeze it, and bring it back to Orlando, where we share it with some of our friends from North Carolina."

As much as Woodruff enjoys the barbecue, it is not his favorite dish. "Ralph's Brunswick stew is the best I have ever had, and that includes the stew served in Brunswick, Georgia."

Like Woodruff, I love barbecue and Brunswick stew and also the hushpuppies and banana pudding. But sometimes I like variety

*Ralph's Barbecue
in Weldon*

and quantity. That is why I timed my visit to Ralph's at suppertime, when the buffet line was open. At lunchtime, after 5:00 P.M., and all day Saturday and Sunday, you can sample the country vegetables, fried chicken, barbecue, and other meats. I tested all of Woodruff's favorites, too, and left about $10 poorer with a very full tummy.

Wes Woodruff says that he is not kin to Ralph and Mason Woodruff, who started Ralph's back in 1946. But when you visit, you can check the history with Mason's daughter Kim Amerson, who runs the family restaurant today.

FROM I-95 Take Exit 173 (Weldon/Roanoke Rapids). Head east on US 158 (Julian R. Allsbrook Hwy.). Go 2 blocks. Ralph's will be there waiting for you on the left.

AFTER EATING Visit the Roanoke Canal Trail, which runs for over 7 miles from Water St. in Weldon to the Roanoke Canal Museum at 15 Jackson St. in Roanoke Rapids.

Afterword

Now that you and I are at the end of this book, remember Tolstoy's words about all great literature being either "a stranger comes to town" or "a man goes on a journey." Pretend for a few moments that you visited all these eateries with me. So together we have made ourselves strangers in town at more than a hundred different places, and we are now at the end of a very long journey.

Okay, maybe we have not made great literature, but you and I have a bookful of stories together.

Before we part, I want to thank you for being my companion and for joining with me in the joy of adventure, surprise, new acquaintances, and a growing appreciation of the rich diversity of the people of our state—and, of course, of finding real good home-style cooking in so many places.

Let's do it again sometime soon.

Until then,

Thanks!

D. G.

Acknowledgments

Warm thanks to the folks at UNC Press, especially the book's editor, Lucas Church, and his assistant, Andrew Winters, who made my work better at every turn, and Mark Simpson-Vos, who persuaded me to undertake this venture. My college classmate Bob Auman read every word several times and made great suggestions about new places to consider. Randy Gardner found many of the new eateries for this revision. Former editors Mary Best and Vicky Jarrett of *Our State* magazine and the others there encouraged me to visit and write about local eateries for their wonderful publications.

This book is the collective effort of countless people who gave me tips about their favorite places, who read selections from the book, who took me to restaurants all over the state, and who encouraged me to continue and complete this project. Some of them are listed here: Shelia Kay Adams, Gene Adcock, Bob Anthony, Chris Arvidson, Bob and Pat Ashley, Phil Baddour, Alton Balance, Hugh and Brenda Barger, Dr. Ben Barker, Cynthia and Robert Bashford, Bobby Benton, Jack Betts, Mark Bibbs, Scott Bigelow, Catherine Bishir, Charles Blackburn, John Blythe, Al Brand, Amy Brandon, Michelle Brooks, Gray Brookshire, David Brown, Stephen Bryant, Tom Bryers, Cliff and Linda Butler, Cindy Campbell, Donna Campbell, Cookie Cantwell, Pete Chikes, Mike Clayton, Charles Coble, George Couch, Ricky Cox, John Curry, Frank Daniels, Gene Davis, Jan and Jim Dean, Don DeArmon, CJ Denny, Henry Doss, Dick Eaker, Jim Early, Rufus Edmisten, Marion Ellis, Bob Epting, Georgann Eubanks, Marcie Ferris, Stephanie Glaser, Stephen

Gletcher, Charles and Katherine Frazier, Bob Garner, May Jo P. Godwin, John Goodman, Margie and Tom Haber, Joe Hackney, Speed Hallman, Jennifer Harris, Thomas Hazel, Patti Head, Tommy Hedrick, Suzanne Hobbs, Charles Holland, Judy Honeycutt Hefner, Darrell Horne, Elizabeth Hudson, Dick Huffman, Jack and Ruby Hunt, Judy Hunt, Judge Bob Hunter, Hugh Johnson, Betty Kenan, Tom Kenan, Fred Kiger, Myrtle Kiker, Mal King, John Kuykendall, Betsy Kylstra, Barbara Ledford, William Ivey Long, Bernie Mann, Janie Matthews, Jamie May, Brake Maynard, Jill McCorkle, Bill McCoy, Stewart McLeod, Grant McRorie, Ruth Mennitt, Moreton Neal, Vernon Neece, Ray Oehler, Nancy Olson, Doug Orr, Joseph Oxendine, Josie Patton, David Perry, Ed Phifer, Judge Dickson Phillips, Julian Pleasants, Hal Powell, Norfleet Pruden, Allan Pugh, John Railey, John Shelton Reed, Pat Colson Reid, Ken Ripley, Wyndham Robertson, John Rogers, Richard Rogers, former judge and UNC System president Tom Ross, Professor Tom E. Ross, Sally and David Royster, Marsden Sale, Raleigh Shoemaker, Lee Smith, Moyer Smith, William Smith, Dick Spangler, Dwight Sparks, Bryan Stabler, John Staples, Shannon Kennedy Stephenson, Shelby Stephenson, Tammy Tingle, Walter Turner, Daniel Wallace, Marcia Webster, Andrea Weigl, Emily and David Weil, Jessica Bradley Wells, Connie Williams, Jerry Williams, Bob Woodruff, Thad Woody, Nancy Wykle, and Lynn York.

If I left you off the list, I owe you a meal at one of the eateries in this book.

D. G. Martin was host of UNC-TV's *NC Bookwatch*, the state's premier literary series from 1999 to 2021, when the final episode aired. A graduate of Davidson College and Yale Law School and a former Green Beret, Martin practiced law in Charlotte for 20 years before joining the University of North Carolina, where he served as vice president for public affairs and chief legislative liaison. Since his retirement he has served in interim leadership positions at UNC-Pembroke, North Carolina Central University, Trust for Public Land, Triangle Land Conservancy, and North Carolina's Clean Water Management Trust Fund and as president of the William R. Kenan Jr. Fund. About 40 North Carolina newspapers carry his weekly column, which features books, politics, and related topics.

Other **Southern Gateways Guides** you might enjoy

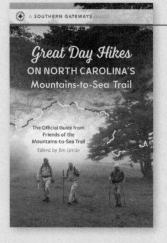